OUT OF CONFLICT

An Autobiography

Françoise Bratt

Date of Publication:
March 2003

Published by:
Guy Bratt
Gerrards Cross,
Buckinghamshire SL9 8PR

ISBN: 0 9524984 1 3

Printed by:
ProPrint
Riverside Cottage
Great North Road
Stibbington
Peterborough PE8 6LR

For my husband, whose intrusion into my life when I was 19 changed the course of it totally, and for our children and grandchildren who resulted from that intrusion.

CONTENTS

FOREWORD

Françoise Bratt, née Girardet, was born in Paris in 1925. Following the outbreak of the Second World War, her life took a totally unexpected direction and, in 1999, her daughter persuaded her to write her memoirs. That she has remained incorrigibly French through more than 55 years of marriage to an uncompromisingly English Englishman is demonstrated by her idiosyncratic and sometimes hilarious English.

The discerning reader may notice that some passages look suspiciously if they had been written by a native English speaker. The explanation is that the author's manuscript was written partly in French, partly in English and partly in a mixture of the two. The first and the third obviously had to be translated and the second 'adjusted' to make the whole generally comprehensible. Also, to maintain continuity, several gaps needed filling. Her husband has done his best to meet these requirements without interfering more than necessary with her charismatic and quirky style.

EARLY YEARS

I was born in 1925 in Neuilly sur Seine, just outside the Paris city boundary, and lived there most of each year until I married. My parents had inherited the family house at Houlgate (between Deauville and Cabourg, in Normandy) and we used to go there for Easter and the months of July and August; September was spent with an aunt and uncle and our cousins at Seppey, near Lausanne in the Canton of Vaud in Switzerland. My father, Robert Girardet, was the youngest of six children; they came from a long line of engravers and painters, dating from the XVIIth century, in Le Locle near Neuchâtel in Switzerland. They were Calvinists. He was born in France so he was a dual national. My grandfather, Eugène, a painter in the Impressionist period, was better known as an "Orientalist"; he had two distinct styles of painting: one of the Norman countryside and the other of Algeria. He was lucky in that he had a rich wife, so he could just enjoy life and paint without having to sell his pictures and this is the reason why he is not very well known; to me, his works of the first style are as good as those of Boudin, Manet, Monet, Corot and Pissaro. These were actually friends of his and it is known that this group would often meet in Normandy and paint. The light and play of natural colours in that part of the world, especially on the coast, are quite renowned. The works of the second style are most impressive for their renderings of the strong light of North Africa. There is quite a demand for them now. These were done at the time when photography was beginning to take over

"Realism" and therefore to be able to be part of a new movement at that time must have been very exciting. My father probably inherited his share of his father's talent; he could draw well and became an electrical engineer but never painted.

Villa Girardet (later called 28 Bd. des Belges), Houlgate

He was a trooper in a French cavalry regiment in World War I. His squadron was wiped out when it was ordered to charge a German machine gun position. He survived because his appendix burst and he fell off his horse into a ditch and, miraculously, lived after having been picked up when, later in the day, the French recaptured the bit of land where he lay. Invalided out of the army, he became a test pilot for his cousin, Louis Bréguet, the aircraft designer. After that, although trained as an electrical engineer, he worked for the rest of his life as the commercial manager of a printing and publishing house, where he had two secretaries with quite ridiculous names: Mme. Pommepourrie (Rotten Apple) and Mlle. Poirecuite. (Cooked Pear)

My mother was the eldest of three children of an English dental surgeon and was by blood 1/2 English, 1/4 Dutch and 1/4 German. Her father practiced half the year in Paris and half in London. He was quite distinguished as one of the earliest dental surgeons and in that capacity he looked after King Edward VII. He earned a very good living but died of a heart attack, brought about by a fall, at 52, leaving a young widow, still in her thirties, who, with her sister, had been at school at a fashionable convent in Ealing, where she made many international contacts who later became patients of her husband and it was one of those who introduced my parents to each other. My mother adored her father and was quite devastated by his death; my grandmother gave the impression of competing with her daughters and would never leave them alone. She never remarried. My mother was a good-looking auburn-haired woman, always impeccably well-dressed, spoilt, obstinate, impatient and used to getting her own way in everything, but at the end of her life she showed immense courage, as appears below.

While my mother was undoubtedly her father's favorite, her sister, Liliane, was equally clearly her mother's. This was very obvious in our grandmother's treatment of us grand-children.

My mother's brother Jean, youngest of the three, was a good-looking playboy, but he loved the sea. He tried to join the Royal Navy in World War I, but was too young; at the outbreak of World War II he succeeded in joining although by this time very nearly too old. He had a gallant war; his ship was sunk but he just survived and in convalescence he was looked after by our English aunt in Yorkshire. Then, when the war was over, he went back to live in France and settled down in Antibes. As a job he was a salesman for the firm Fulmen, selling batteries for cars. As he loved the sea and was a good sailor, he decided to use a sailing boat instead of a car to visit his customers all along the Mediterranean Coast. He had a charming girl-friend (Mme. Weil), who was a superb cook and loved him dearly, but she was extremely "dépensière" (spendthrift) and loved luxurious goods and a luxurious life which my dear uncle could not afford, but they managed their life very well: her husband was a very rich and successful Parisian lawyer, so she commuted from Paris to Antibes every other week. This satisfied everybody, apart from Aunt Liliane, who purported to be shocked by his behaviour and never wanted to talk to him again.

I thought he was terrific, good looking, charming, entertaining, and he and his friend who both threw fabulous parties in their beautiful villas were also great friends of Cocteau and Somerset Maugham.

My brother Olivier – four years older than me – and I had a happy and carefree childhood. We were not encouraged by our parents to work at school, and I, indeed, was sometimes prevented from doing my homework, so as not to give Olivier a complex. It was taken for granted that he would, without any qualifications, slip into my father's firm at the top level and that I would marry a suitable husband of my parents' choice. His specifications were to be rich, bourgeois or better, mindful of the importance of "les apparences", respectful and obedient to his mother-in-law and Protestant (unless really very rich indeed). Our parents had met at a party in Paris 1919. At that time the survivors of World War I, which had inflicted such terrible casualties on French males, were determined to enjoy life fully, without much thought about anything else. For this reason, children of the bourgeoisie of my age hardly saw their parents. Servants, upon whom so much depended, were badly paid and treated like slaves.

This way of life, surprisingly, continued until 1936, when Leon Blum's Popular Front Government introduced " Obligatory Paid Holidays". Even after this date the bourgeoisie had a very comfortable and easy life until the outbreak of World War II. Hence my carefree childhood. I have always had happy memories of those summer holidays. When we were in Switzerland with my cousins, we used to go fishing for crayfish in small rivers nearby. We children were sent out by the parents to collect "chanterelles", but rarely ate any because our parents loved them and there were never enough left over for us. We used to play hide and seek in the big barns full of hay in the two farms nearby. Sometimes we would help the farmers to collect the potatoes in the fields. One of these farms had an outside bread oven and the smell of new bread coming out of the oven was marvellous and has stayed with me all these years until now.

I was the only girl with five boys, so I had to defend myself fiercely. One of the five, Michel, exactly the same age as me, used to exasperate me, particularly and especially when he sucked up to our grandmother. When I commented on this one day he said: "Yes, but look how well it works". Eventually I got my own back. Seeing him sitting on the wall of the lane, opposite the stand-pipe of the liquid manure tank, I opened the tap and a powerful, foul-smelling jet drenched him and knocked him off the wall. He stank for days. On the whole, we had lots of fun, we used to have 2 or 3 wooden carts which we connected together and went down hill on narrow lanes at terrific speed; it is amazing that none of us ever broke any bones. There was one other cousin, Jean; one very hot day he annoyed me so much that we fought and, to escape me, he ran to grab a branch to take refuge in a tree. I managed to pull his pants down and threw them on a manure heap – he was stuck in the tree, naked, without trousers and too shy to come down – unfortunately for me, his mother, when she discovered what had happened, reported the incident to my mother, so I was punished and sent to my room without dinner, but it was worth it – we laughed so much – and many years later when we met again, we talked about this incident and he also remembered it vividly. But on the whole when I look back at what we were doing, we had a wonderful happy childhood. When this event took place we must have been about eight years old.

Another memory of about that time concerns a family named Costille, great friends of my parents. They spent alternating periods in Paris and Rio De Janeiro until World War II broke out, when they stayed in Brazil until it was over. They had made a vast fortune from their huge coffee plantation and lived in a large and beautiful flat on the 6th floor in Bd. Henri Martin, near the Trocadero. In the hall there was an enormous bird-cage, so big that one could stand up inside it, and it contained many beautiful and rare birds and a parrot, who used to call me funny names. The Costilles had one child, a daughter named Monique, the same age as me, and whenever they were in Paris I used to go to their flat on Thursdays (there was no school on Thursdays) to play. She was very spoilt and had lots of games but was very clumsy and neither sporty nor courageous. I used to slide down the banisters from the 6th to the ground floor where I had to slow down and stop before hitting a huge bronze ball which would have done me no good. Of course I was used to doing this but if I had slipped, I would have fallen down the stair well and undoubtedly killed myself. Monique just watched. She also just watched when I let down 25 centime coins, which had holes in the middle, on a long thread from the balcony to the pavement and caused passers-by to wonder what was going on when the coins took off and disappeared upwards. The hall in that flat was paved with marble and I used to love to tap dance; it made a terrific noise but Monique had no idea how to do it.

Sadly, every Thursday for lunch there were bananes flambées au Rhum which I could not stand and was immediately sick at the end of the meal but I was too shy to say that I did not like them. Before the war for all the time I knew her, every second year they came to live in their beautiful flat in Paris for 6 months and during this period they enjoyed themselves to the full. As they had lots of money they gave lots of parties and my parents were always invited to these parties and told us everything that went on.

My parents also were good bridge players and, night after night, if they were not playing bridge, they went to dinners in the most fashionable restaurants in Paris at that time, followed by night clubs. They had survived the first World War and they were going to enjoy their lives to the full. They were right if they could do it and they were so lucky to have such wonderful and fun friends, who liked them very much and invited them very often. I had left France when I married and by that time Monique had been married and divorced and had no children. Before the war broke out, our life in Paris was very pleasant. I had lots of fun being a "Petite Eclaireuse (Brownie)" from the age of 7 until 14. About 20 of us would gather every Thursday morning at the vestry of the Protestant church in Neuilly. We were then taken to the Bois de Boulogne to play lots of games and in the spring we were taken to the swimming pool on the Seine. We were taught dancing, needlework, painting, and religious studies. We used to play tennis most Saturdays and that was fun because, when the summer holidays arrived, we went to Houlgate and there I could really enjoy myself and play lots more tennis during July and August. When I saw Monique after the war in 1954 we had nothing left in common and we did not keep in touch after that. Both her parents had died of natural causes in about 1960 in Brazil. My parents were very sad indeed as the Costilles had been a part of their lives, which had vanished. However these fantastic memories were left to them. So I climbed trees and, later, mountains, rode horses, played tennis, skied, and was taught dress-making by the obligatory family dress-maker, Mme Chevalier, who came one day a week. I did lots of gymnastics and wanted to be trained as a ballet dancer. This was not allowed because respectable bourgeois young ladies did not do that.

Then World War II started. I was 14½.

PARIS - SEPTEMBER 1939-1942

With war impending, we realized that our lives were going to change but for the time being we stayed in Houlgate. All our friends were there too so, instead of taking us as usual to Switzerland, to my cousins' house in Seppey in September, my father thought it was wiser to stay put. A few days after having taken that decision, the war broke out. My parents decided to stay in Houlgate but my father had to go to Paris because he was mobilized in the Defence of Paris by barrage balloons, which were put up in the sky in the hope of preventing air bombardments. That did not last long and he was demobilized and went back to the printing works where he had worked since 1920. So in that first year, until spring 1940, he used to commute by train from Paris to Houlgate every other weekend. Mother organized their life in Houlgate, playing lots of bridge with all their friends and she organized some cooking lessons two mornings a week because in those days most of the women of the bourgeoisie had cooks, so, when the war came and they realised that they would have to economize, they thought they had better learn to cook. My poor mother, even after taking the classes, had no idea how to cook, but her sister, Aunt Liliane, was a little more gifted and, owing to her, we survived until the spring of 1940.

During this period we went to school in Houlgate with all our friends. The lycée in Caen sent some teachers and there were enough of us to have classes from 6ème to the baccalauréat. We actually did learn quite a lot, but we had lots of fun.

Every weekend, we organized hockey matches at the Sarlabot Golf Club which was in a beautiful position on the top of a hill overlooking the sea and Houlgate. We used to go up there by bike which was tough up hill but great coming down; generally after these matches four of us used to go to my friend Monique Burckhardt's house to have tea. The tea was served by a butler, which was quite incredible at that time; we listened to music and sometimes danced. I will never forget those few months of the phoney war. We were having so much fun and I am so glad we had that fun, because afterwards everything changed dramatically and we did not have any fun at all until the war was over and Paris was liberated in August 1944.

One morning in June 1940, we woke up to find the sky completely dark. The French authorities had blown up the petrol depots at Le Havre to stop them falling into the hands of the Germans. Lots of refugees from the north of France were coming through Houlgate; most of the cars passing in front of our house had mattresses on their roofs and we wondered why. We soon realized it was to try to protect those inside from the machine-gun bullets which the Germans fired from their planes. They flew low down and when they saw lines of cars on the roads they opened fire on them; we were terribly frightened to hear this news and the people looked haggard. One car stopped in front of our house. On the back seat lay one of their children who had been hit by machine-gun fire and lay there dead, but the parents would not abandon him. It was dreadful to watch this poor family, and they were not by any means the only ones in that condition.

When we saw that the people from the north of France were leaving their towns to get away from the Germans, we thought that at any moment Le Havre would be under attack and the Germans would soon be in Houlgate. It was at this time that we received a sharp reminder of the size and ubiquity of the German Fifth Column in France: the owner of a garage near Houlgate appeared on his forecourt wearing a German uniform. So my mother, my brother, some friends and I left Houlgate in a convoy of about six cars. We stayed together as far as the Loire and then separated. North of the Loire we were twice machine-gunned but fortunately escaped injury because we heard the planes coming and jumped out of the cars and dived into ditches to take cover. We were for a terrifyingly long time stuck on a bridge over the Loire because the traffic was so heavy, but we made it safely just before the bridge was destroyed by bombs and some of the unfortunates on it were drowned. A few hours later we met my father in a town called Cholet. The meeting place was a small hotel run by the father of the cook whom my mother had employed for many years before these terrible events took place. The next day we left in convoy, Father and I in his car and Mother and my brother in hers. We had three jerry cans of petrol which my father's brother Jacques had brought with him and we reached Biarritz and went to the house of uncle Jacques who was the finance director of his cousin, Louis Bréguet's, firm, which had moved from Villacoubley, outside Paris, to avoid the Germans, and established itself at Anglet, not far from Biarritz.

There were many people everywhere and the traffic was thick. People thought the French army would surely stop the Germans at the Loire, as they had not done so at the Seine, but a few days after we got to Biarritz a German Panzer formation arrived. Many Jewish families were desperate. They wanted to flee to Spain; many did, but many were arrested. We stayed with my cousins for about three weeks. They lived in a large house, so fortunately there was plenty of room for us. We were all bewildered and wondered what we should do. Lots of people, especially Jewish families, were aiming for Bordeaux to try to go to England.

It became clear to us that we could not go anywhere else, so we decided to head back to Paris and this took quite some time due to the movement of German troops, especially the tank regiments, which for days occupied all the main roads of France. They allowed a few cars at a time to do a few kilometers and then we had to stop to allow their tanks through. It took us a very long time to reach Paris; we had to stay in Genillé near Tours, at a family friend's house, for nearly two weeks to keep off the road. Trying to find petrol was a nightmare as there was already a shortage. We heard at that time that France would have a French Government and not be made into a German Province. We heard also that France would be divided in two, the northern part occupied by the Germans and the southern part not. As my grandmother on my mother's side was English, we thought it would be safer for her to stay in unoccupied France, so she went to live in Nice next door to some friends of hers. We went back to Paris, but we were worried about my brother who was 17, because the Germans wanted to have French workers for their factories. Fortunately it took the Germans over a year after they had invaded our country to start trying to round up the French men; by then lots of them had disappeared into hiding and started the Resistance. My brother was passed along an escape chain by the Resistance and then escaped through Spain to North Africa. We had no news from him for 2 years. It was very sad for me and for my parents, too; we had no idea if he was alive or not. We learnt later that he went through a terrible time. He was arrested in Spain and put into the horrible prison camp of Miranda, where lots of young men died of dysentery. The few who survived were freed and exchanged for big loads of flour which the American government sent to the Spaniards. Fortunately he survived and managed to find his way to Morocco. There he joined the French Commando's Parachute Battalion. They later landed in the South of France and it was at that point we heard that he was alive. What a joy that was for all of us. Unfortunately a few months later he was badly wounded in the head when carrying out a very dangerous mission for which he had volunteered. When it seemed certain that he would not survive, he was recommended for a Médaille Militaire, which carries a pension with it. When, thanks to an immense effort by our father, Olivier was removed to a Paris hospital and survived, the citation was cancelled. A senior officer named d'Astier de la Vigèrie was outraged by this and fought for some 15 years to get it reinstated and eventually succeeded. But Olivier was never to be the same as before. Later, after my marriage, he was pushed by our parents to marry a perfectly dreadful, mad girl because she was Protestant and purported to be very rich. This was even more sad.

Olivier became estranged from our parents and from me and I lost contact with him entirely for the last 14 years of his life. My cousin Michel, to whom I referred so disparagingly above, took the first opportunity, which was in Strasbourg, to join the "Spahis" (French regiment formed in North Africa) and was later badly wounded in the left arm, but survived the war and we are very good friends. He and his wife live in their old family house in Seppey. Now, whenever we go to Switzerland we always call on them there.

In October 1941 I started to cough and run a slight temperature every morning. I felt tired and began to lose weight. After a few weeks of this, I was x-rayed, which showed a slight shadow on one lung. Immediately our doctor told my parents that I must leave Paris and be sent to the mountains. This meant crossing the "ligne de démarcation" from the occupied part of France to the unoccupied, which entailed much form-filling and bureaucracy to get a permit to travel. I was sent to Mégève, to a finishing school called Les Fauvettes, where they took young girls with health troubles which were not difficult to cure. I, for example, only needed fresh air and good food which we did not have in Paris. After 4 weeks I was fit again, but it was decided that I should stay six months. So when winter came, we managed to ski at least three times a week and every weekend. I learnt cooking, dress-making and philosophy(!) The daughter of great friends of my mother's came to join me and spend the semester there. As she lived in Nice it was easy for her to get to Mégève because Nice was also in the unoccupied zone. Her name was Nicole Larue. My cousin Pierre Bréguet (son of

Louis Bréguet) was at this time working at the Bréguet factory at Anglet near Biarritz and, having had a bad dose of influenza, he came to see me in Mégève and, at the same time, have a long weekend in the mountains to recover. I introduced him to Nicole and they fell in love. Pierre came back more and more often and a year later they were married, so Nicole owed me a debt to which I shall refer again later.

The Germans had requisitioned several hotels in Mégève, as a leave centre for the troops from the Russian front. When we saw them on the slopes, they all wore their white camouflage uniforms used in the Russian winter. They all looked tired and very sad and, near the end of their periods of leave, they all skied like mad things, in the hope of breaking a limb to avoid being sent back to Russia.

Shortly after the end of my six months stay at Les Fauvettes, it closed because the woman who ran it did not understand the system of allocation of ration coupons and had used them all up, leaving herself none for future months.

At the beginning of the German occupation, from 1940 to 1942, the Germans did everything possible to be friendly with us; they even had orders from Hitler himself to be chivalrous. They tried to ingratiate themselves with French families so as to be invited in and could not understand why they were not welcome and very few families accepted them, especially in my circle of friends. This is one reason why we never danced or played dance music records because, if the Germans heard this sort of music, they wanted to come and enjoy the fun and gatecrash the gathering. So instead of dancing we learned to play bridge and during the four years of occupation we played and played. This game has again become an important component of my life in my old age.

Also, at mid-day every day during those four years of the occupation, the Germans held a parade, led by a military band, which marched down the Champs Elysés from the Arc de Triomphe to the Place de la Concorde. This continued for a time after the allied landing in Normandy but was abruptly stopped when RAF fighters, by then enjoying complete air superiority, after warning the population by dropping leaflets, machine-gunned the marchers and caused casualties.

PARIS – LAST YEARS OF THE OCCUPATION, 1942-44

From 1942 onwards things started to change. The Germans were not so victorious any more and their attitude of conquerors and the smugness of being in power were not to last much longer. The United States entered the war in 1942 and, in spite of the Nazis' efforts to suppress it, the bad news from the Russian front became public knowledge. Many Germans were murdered in the streets with the result that reprisals increased. No-one was safe out in the streets, whole blocks of innocent passers-by would be rounded up, taken hostage, arrested, sent to work camps or sometimes shot, depending on the whim of the officer in charge. Life was on tenter-hooks as to whether so-and-so would get home that evening or ever be seen again, as the rumour would get out that the Germans had rounded up a bunch of people in this neighbourhood or that. Living in constant apprehension became routine. For a young girl of 17 going out with friends would have seemed to be a normal thing to be able to do. However, since the Germans' arrival, freedom of fun for the young did not exist. If I went out and did not return close to the time expected, my parents were convinced I'd been arrested. Worries of parents had never been more extreme than at that time. As parents, you had to allow for bomb alerts and metro delays and give children time margins for their tardiness. However, some parents, whose children were working for the Resistance and who had no idea they were doing so, were never to see their offspring again. The realities of loss and sheer uselessness were never felt more strongly than during that period. Dancing or just visiting friends in the evening was not possible. In our crowd of friends many worked for the Resistance and many disappeared; they died under torture or were sent to camps to die. To put it mildly, we grew up very fast, accepting losses of those so dear to one in those turbulent developing years; teenagers of today are totally tame in comparison. It was not unusual for the Nazis brutally to torture Resistance workers to obtain information, often involving the prisoner's girl-friend or boy-friend to add to their torment. I had a very dear childhood friend, a medical student, Pascal de Brunoff, who worked for the Resistance. The Gestapo caught him and tortured him. When he refused to speak they cut out his tongue. Then they took me to see him. Then they shot him. This gratuitous brutality marked me for life and I still have reservations about even the nicest Germans I have met over the years.

As in all wars or occupied zones, food was rationed. We were lucky at the beginning of the war and were able to maintain a reasonable diet but by 1942 things had changed drastically. Thanks to my mother, who had friends, the Aumonts, who lived in Normandy and owned a farm, we used to receive a food package – consisting of a tin box which was filled and sent by post once a week and returned empty – with such rarities as butter, an unheard of luxury in those years. This little game lasted until the middle of 1942, when the Germans became more and more suspicious of everything going by post and soon terminated such missives. From then on until the end of the occupation we never saw butter again. Food became scarcer – it was not unusual to go to bed hungry and not eat a decent meal for several weeks. An example of this starvation was experienced by some friends of my parents, Madeleine Rey and her husband Marcel. The latter was always hungry. One day, when Madeleine was out playing bridge, Marcel came home, hungry as usual, and went straight to the fridge to see if he could find something to get his teeth into. He caught sight of something in a bowl on the kitchen table. It looked like yogurt, so he added his customary dose of sugar and ate it. A few minutes later Madeleine arrived and went straight to the kitchen to find the bowl, but it was nowhere to be seen. She asked Marcel if he had seen it and explained that before going out she had removed the kitchen curtains, ersatz of course, which were filthy and had put them to soak in soapy water - also ersatz (soap and wood chips). They had naturally all disintegrated into a porridge-looking mess, which Marcel had taken for a pudding. Thereupon he had to be rushed off to hospital to have his stomach pumped. Hilarious in retrospect but not at all funny at the time.

Ration coupons were issued from town halls but they did not provide enough food to live on; everyone made whatever arrangements they could to obtain a little extra. We had a great piece of luck. Mme Chevalier, the family dress-maker referred to above, lived in rue Cardinet in the XVe arrondissement, an area which was home to many of the prostitutes who consorted with German soldiers and were paid for their services, in part, with powdered eggs, soap, sometimes bananas and oranges. The prostitutes sold these delicacies to a hairdresser who sold them to Mme Chevalier who, in turn, sold them to us. My mother and I went to rue Cardinet on our bicycles twice a month to collect whatever was available.

The winters of 1942 and 1943 were particularly and unforgettably wretched. They were very cold and we had no means of heating other than one open fire-place in the drawing room. My father used to bring home old telephone directories from his office and we burned them, as slowly as possible, in that fire-place, to try to have a little warmth for as long as we could. Damp ran down all the walls in our flat; I used to cover my bed with newspapers to try to keep my bed-clothes dry but I suffered from chilblains on my hands and feet.

There was no question of entertaining or having a party to celebrate any event. I had the idea of making an imitation birthday-cake for my father's 48th birthday. I soaked some newspapers in water and made them into a ball, mixed in some plaster and flattened the result into a sort of thick wafer. When it was dry, I covered it with some more plaster and stuck some candles into it. The spectacular product brought me congratulations from everyone and I tried to cut it into slices, but that unfortunately did not work. The only thing that remained was the memory of my father's birthday that year.

One's teeth and hair suffered terribly. A visit to the dentist was not recommended unless really essential. No local anaesthetics were available and I remember being tied down like in a strait jacket to have some infected impacted wisdom teeth wrenched out. Passing out in the dentist's chair was the best anaesthetic , oh! but wait for the recovery pain. You can imagine the never-ending throbbing.

It was at this time, whilst still at the lycée studying for the bachot, that I was contacted by one of the Resistance groups. The Resistance worked in small cells which were tightly organized and very tight-lipped about who was with whom. This, of course, was to protect themselves from being discovered, should someone under torture divulge identities. Inflicting torture was a favorite pass-time of the Nazis, especially from 1942 till the end of the German occupation. I was asked to become a courier across Paris. I would be told to drop off letters at a certain mail box at a certain time; I would never know the content, the identity of the correspondents or the urgency of these missives. The drop-offs would be quite irregular; you never knew when you were going to be called upon to do your bit. The hatred we had for the Germans was so violent that you did what you could to get your own back and you would guard, literally with your life, the letter which you were carrying; you shared with your cell the conviction that all this was against a common enemy. So I would pedal my bike through check points with some missive or other stashed away in my books, in my pump, anywhere, and, to my joy, undetected. I managed to pass on about 60 letters for the common cause. You can imagine the wobbling knees at check points but the Germans were so unobservant. One's heart pounded so loudly and so fast that one would think a whole city block would hear the thumping. The success of these acts of defiance was the beginning of the end for the Germans.

It was in 1942 that my father managed to build a wireless. It was fitted in the bathroom, furthest from the neighbours' walls. At last we could hear broadcasts from

London – "La France Libre". This was very beneficial to our state of mind, seeing that until then we heard only German propaganda and at that time the Germans were set on announcing that the English were done for and that there was no hope for them. Hearing the English and free French broadcasts was like icing on the cake for us. It was at that time that my brother went missing, on his way to join the Free French forces in north Africa. Somehow, as I explained before, we had faith that he was alive. Getting any additional information gave the family encouragement and in due course we got word of his whereabouts.

At this point I have a flash back to six incidents worth recounting. The first three took place in the Metro. One day I was with a wild friend (who, I think now, must have been border line nuts), in the usual crowdedness of a Paris Metro train, with civilians and German troops. Two German sailors were standing in front of my friend and me, with their backs to us. You must understand that the German sailors wore hats with long ribbons hanging down their backs. Well, this was too much for my friend who was standing behind the post behind them. She reached for their ribbons and tied them around the post in front of her without their knowing or feeling any thing. My eyes nearly fell out their sockets at the sight of this prank and the civilians all around us could not believe the nerve of this girl and envisaged a reprisal for this lack of respect the Germans. No one said a thing. The Metro was pulling into a station and you could see everyone getting restless, ready to rush out of the doors as soon as they opened. To the familiar humming sound of the stationary train, everyone dashed out and the sailors made as if to do the same but inevitably knocked their heads together and swore. This happened and the doors closed so fast for the Metro to continue its journey that there was no time to sound the alarm and round up hostages for disciplinary action. I suppose my friend got kicks out of the sheer audacity of seeing how far she could go. The scary thing was that, in her youthfulness, she did not realize that she was putting so many at risk.

The second story, involving the same friend, goes something like this. One day she came up to me very excited and said. "I must show you my latest collection" and she opened up a folder into which she had attached small square pieces of material. I looked more closely and realized that they were samples cut out from German uniforms, each piece representing possibly a different uniform. She told me that the Metro was her source for the collection and that she carried on with her "job" under the noses of everyone and no-one ever told her to stop. I could only imagine the fellow Metro passengers holding their breath and jumping out at the first possible stop. This friend was the daughter of a very well-known Protestant Pastor, Pasteur Monod, and my friend was an eccentric, atheist and very turbulent; she was finally caught by the Germans and was extremely lucky to survive. Her father had apparently been able to negotiate her release.

The third story is about my aged great-aunt, Mme Fenwick, who was rather lame and walked with a stick. She made a habit of tripping Germans up just at the moment when they were getting out of the Metro and the doors already closing. As the train moved off, with her victims falling about outside, she would say to all around: "Ah, that is my fifth (or whatever) today". She always managed to time her action just right and was never caught.

The fourth story I want to tell is about students having a bit of fun. In restaurants it was customary for the Germans to hang up their belts, with small arms, on the clothes hooks near the tables or even by the door. Well, the students would hang up their belts attached to which would be their bicycle pumps. The sight of the innocence and death in one quick glance made such a strong visual impact that it is hard to forget it.

The fifth story is about a rather thick German officer who, on leaving his hotel every morning, bought a newspaper from a kiosk nearby. Each day the news vendor would hand him the paper with the words: "Tiens, voilà, grand con" (con is a very rude word for an egregious imbecile). After a time the officer got around to wondering what this daily remark meant and asked a Frenchman, who explained that it was an abbreviation for "conquérant". So, next morning, the officer replied to the news vendor's customary greeting: "Non. Moi je suis un petit con, Hitler est un grand con".

Finally, I must add that one night at the Theatre de 10 Heures (a theatre known for its political satire) in Paris in 1943, an actor came scurrying on to the stage at the beginning of the scene, one arm lifted in the Heil Hitler pose and said in a loud voice " Je reviens de ma campagne où il y a de la merde haut comme ça partout (I've just returned from my place in the country where there is shit as high as THIS everywhere!)". This raised a roar of laughter from all the non-Germans in the house.

Several German officers sitting in the front row got up and promptly arrested the actor, who then spent three months in jail.

I had a close friend at school named Pauline Cohen. In 1942 the Germans enforced their "cleansing" of the Jews in Paris. As these raids got more intensive, on my way to school I would say to her as we walked down the street together: "Why don't you and your brothers and sisters and parents try to leave?" She would reply: " You see my father, my grand father and my uncles have always been here, they have been jewellers for generations and this is our home, like it is yours, this is where their life is." One day I did not see her on the way to school, I did not see her in class nor during break in the courtyard. I found out that she and her whole family had been arrested and sent to Auschwitz where every single one of them died. For 16 year olds to be confronted with those types of horrors and realities of what was happening around us caused us to grow up very fast emotionally during those occupation years. Our youth was splintered by the realisation of what nastiness mankind is capable. One only has to hear about animals like Saddam Hussein or Milosevic, 50 years later, to be aware that people like that still exist and threaten and not only tolerate but require such evil behaviour from their followers.

From 1942 onwards the Germans were more and more worried, nervous and aggressive until the end of the war. Their behaviour changed and general attitudes towards the Parisians became very disturbing and unpredictable. I remember being at the Printemps department store on Boulevard Haussman in the centre of Paris one day. Suddenly shots rang out, the doors of the shop were closed (as was customary whenever the Germans needed to investigate an incident to find the culprit) and shouts were heard. Fifteen German policemen were at the scene very quickly and their hunt for the culprit was on: a German officer had been shot. I knew instinctively that the Resistance were behind this deed and that the assassin would have managed to escape before the closing of the shop doors; I also knew that the Germans would take hostages in reprisal so I had to think quickly. I was standing in the fur department so I had the idea of hiding inside a long coat. I stayed there for what felt like half the day, hardly daring to breathe and listening to the shouts and trying to understand what was going on. Then I heard some footsteps approaching in my direction and immediately I thought I had been discovered. Fortunately they passed by me and I could relax; a few seconds later I heard them again and the fact that their owners were speaking German confirmed that they were soldiers or military police. Again I stopped breathing; this time, I thought, I have been discovered, but no, they passed me again and went away. By that time I was drenched with sweat and exhausted by such emotions and I shall always remember those terrible few minutes as if they were yesterday. Then, slowly and very carefully, I crept out and peered over the banisters to try to see something or someone. Then I saw a sales assistant who said: "They took ten people randomly from each floor. You did well to hide: those people will almost certainly be arrested and sent to some camp. No doubt the assassin has gone free".

These random assassinations were really very stupid. They served no purpose and it was the innocent population who got the blame. Often the acts were committed by individuals seeking personal revenge on the Germans. Had they realized the terrible consequences of their deeds many reprisals could have been avoided and lives spared. But the hatred for the Germans was so strong that people acted in the most irresponsible ways.

Throughout the occupation the only practical way to get around Paris was by bicycle. Thanks to those two-wheelers we were able to have a bit of freedom. You could go out at night until 10 p.m. but invariably had to stay over night because of the strict curfew laws; if you were outside after that time you'd be arrested, thrown in jail and possibly sent to a concentration camp. Towards the end of the war the tyres on our bikes were totally worn out, so we invented a replacement system, of using wire which was threaded through old corks which were inserted instead of the tube. Not very comfortable but it did the trick.

As mentioned before, everything was in short supply and many things totally unobtainable. My cousin Monique and I became expert at making shoes; we used cork soles and hat felt for the uppers. The felt came from our fathers' old hats. We used razor blades to cut the felt and the end products looked very chic and became very popular. Woe betide you should you be wearing the shoes in the rain...the cork would swell. So from time to time you would see people walking barefoot holding their shoes in their hands during and after a downpour.

The shortage of clothing forced people with any creativity to get very creative indeed with their resources. I remember that my first long dress was made out of some curtains. Many people made charming comments on my attire; little did they know where the material actually came from or what it was really for. The only available fabric was "ersatz", a mixture of wood fibres and cotton. There again one had to be careful not to get rained on as the outfit would shrink. You cannot imagine the Parisiennes without elegant clothes. So even during 1942-43 fashion collections still appeared but the fabric was newsprint and not cotton. In celebration for the Longchamps horse races in May of these years, some women had fun and came out wearing some incredible dresses made of newspaper. One kept fingers crossed that the heavens did not open! It is amazing what vanity will do. It is also amazing to see what creativity can be attained with such limited materials.

At the beginning of 1942, my father was approached in his office by a German officer who wanted him to print some propaganda magazines and pamphlets. He told my father that his name was Girardet, too, and that they must be cousins and therefore he ought to cooperate. My father replied "certainly not, but maybe at the end of the war, if you are still alive, come and see me then and we can talk about the possibility." The German was furious and on leaving did his Heil Hitler salute; my father was outraged and he told us the whole story upon his return home that evening.

It was about that time, too, that my father was approached by a member of the Resistance who asked him if he could help by producing from memory drawings of German gun positions along the Normandy coast where our summer house is in Houlgate; he had seen these in 1941 before it became "zone interdite". He remembered the positions very well and produced a number of important maps which were very useful, due to the detail, during the landing in June 1944.

I was extremely lucky during the winters of the last two years of the occupation as I was allowed to go wild boar hunting on horseback. Wild boar had crossed the Rhine with the Germans and had become such a pest in France that the Germans not only hunted them themselves but also allowed some French people to do so. My best friend, whom I had met at Sunday school when I was 7, Solange Vernes, had a home in the Rambouillet Forest and her father had a number of horses, which somehow were never eaten, and once a week I used to go riding and hunting. This was like an escape and we would forget that a war was going on. We would be riding for six to seven hours without a notion of what was happening outside the forest. The return home through the forest at the end of the hunt was and remains in my memory as an amazing experience. In the silence all you could hear was the crackling of the leaves and sticks under the horses' hooves and the snorts and coughs of the horses after their exertions. The riders were silent and listened to the forest noises – the occasional tapping of a wood-pecker or the scurrying noise of a squirrel caught unaware nibbling on some prize nut. I used to return home to my family with a chunk of meat which we would marinate and this would keep us going for the week.

On the 6th June 1944 – a date that I will not forget – when we awakened we heard a tremendous noise coming from the sky and saw masses and masses of planes dropping leaflets. These leaflets told us of the allied landings in Normandy, the British mainly at and east of Arromanches, the Americans at and west of Omaha Beach. As you can imagine, the atmosphere was very tense, the Germans in the street were unsettled and insecure, civilians were being arrested for doing nothing and one had to make sure to keep out of the way. We, on the other hand, listening more assiduously than ever on my father's home-made wireless to the Free French broadcast and deciphering their more scrambled messages, were ecstatic at the news we heard but had to make sure not to show our joy when we went out into the street. That June/July period was one of great tension. We were constantly wondering what the Germans would do next. We had heard that Hitler had ordered that all the historical monuments in Paris, the bridges and the Metro should be blown up. The St. Cloud tunnel (through which passes the main road out of Paris to the west) which the Germans had already filled with dynamite was also to be destroyed. I continued to bike around the city, as this was the only means of transport; the queues for bread grew longer and longer and when one's turn came the bread one was given was made of a mixture of bran, saw-dust and a minimal amount of rough wheat flour. One had to be starving to eat it. There was no meat, butter or fruit but only a few root vegetables, and some dried vegetables if you were lucky enough to find them.

Troops coming ashore on D-day

We knew what it was like to be really starving but the excitement of imminent freedom kept us going; we were content to be patient and not to complain. Fortunately the weather was beautiful and warm.

Towards the 25 July, the battle of the Plaine de Caen was finally won by the Allies after many casualties on both sides; the more fanatical Germans were ready to die for Hitler, to fight to the last man and not surrender, so the fighting was ferocious. If some German soldiers wanted to surrender they were shot from behind by the SS on their way to do so. During this period, in Paris, we witnessed some little groups of German deserters trying to escape and hide in Paris and when they were discovered by the German Military police they were shot on the spot.

Paris street scene during the liberation.
Note the carefully neutral gendarmes.

I was asked by some friends of mine who were medical students whether I would join with others to help pick up the wounded and I of course agreed. The Germans were gradually losing their grip and getting very trigger-happy and shooting at random into crowds of civilians, killing or wounding many. They would empty their magazines shooting at apartments overlooking the streets and at anything that moved. It was totally unpredictable and unsettling to all. I was then only 18 and it took me a little time to get used to seeing dead bodies. However, it was amazing how quickly one became accustomed to the sight of flowing blood and suffering. I became blasée and just got on as efficiently as I could with the job of picking up the dead and wounded who had been hit for being in the wrong place at the wrong time. The Germans themselves were very scared because they were increasingly attacked by the members of the Resistance and for the civilians it was very tricky because one could easily be caught in the crossfire between the Germans and the Resistance chaps on the street. One really had to be very careful when one went out. Just before the arrival of Général Leclerc, the actual Liberation, there was much more bloodshed on the streets. There were snipers in abundance and they fired into the rejoicing crowds; emotions swung between joy and fear.

We had to take the wounded to various postes de secours (medical shelters) scattered in the different neighbourhoods of Paris. Mine was the Avenue de la Grande Armée (Général de Gaulle) very near to the Arc de Triomphe.

At the beginning of August, we saw some of the Germans arriving from Normandy in vehicles of all sorts camouflaged with branches. They all looked very exhausted and their vehicles all went in different directions because, during the night before they reached Paris, the Resistance had re-arranged all the road signs: there was total traffic chaos everywhere.

On the 25th of August, early in the morning, I was in my poste de secours with my friend Solange. We had been busy late the previous night, having to pick up some civilians who had been shot in the legs by the Germans. When we heard a roaring, clanking noise, coming nearer and nearer, we went out into the street and saw the first tanks of Général Leclerc's Army approaching. It was absolutely fantastic, everybody became completely, madly enthusiastic, some people were crying with joy and it was an extraordinary experience. Unfortunately, lots of these French soldiers were suffering from conjunctivitis and their poor eyes were in a terrible state. We spent our time boiling water, putting salt in it and trying to bathe as many eyes as we could and we did that for 24 hours nonstop. They were so happy to have a bit of relief. At the same time we were asked also to go and get some people who had been shot while looking from their flat windows at the Germans who were trying to escape fighting with the Army Leclerc. They were furious to see people shouting and looking at them, so, in revenge, they fired their machine guns into windows. Lots of people got hurt that way, during that period, which lasted two days, and we were kept very busy. I have never seen so much blood in such a small period of my life and I will never forget it.

The Leclerc Tanks came into Paris up the Avenue de la Grande Armée, so, as I said, we were in the best place to see them all. Some of them were Parisians and when they bivouacked outside our shelter, they asked if they could come in and use the telephone to tell their parents, wives, sisters and girl-friends that they were in Paris. It was incredible to hear all their conversations; they had not heard or seen their families for 4 years and there they were; it was a very moving moment.

It was then that we learnt that General von Choltitz, the German commander in Paris, had been ordered by Hitler to destroy everything. Von Choltitz had ignored the order and Hitler, mad with rage, had ordered him back to Germany for execution. Von Choltitz had refused to go and was persuaded by Raoul Nordling, the Swedish Consul-General, to sign a truce with the Resistance on the 22nd of August for two days. On the 24th he surrendered to General Leclerc and took refuge in the Swedish Consulate-General.

The memory of the arrival of Général Leclerc in Paris on that beautiful August day in 1944 will remain embedded in my mind for ever. The joy in the streets and the relief that it was all over for Paris gave one an amazing feeling. In the air was an atmosphere of partying. One danced with everyone and social boundaries were lowered, the masses were out in force and we were free from the German grip. However, in spite of this incredible sensation, Germans were still in hiding and firing on the crowd from well-chosen hide outs. French collaborators by this time had all slipped away, hoping, no doubt, to get to Germany. It was not uncommon for civilians or liberators to fall under the bullet after a heroic or brilliant war. There were stories of returning French soldiers and Resistance members being shot down just when their goal had been reached and of Americans, who had battled their way on the D-day beaches like Utah, the disastrous Omaha and so on only to glimpse the Eifel tower and be shot by unseen cowards lurking up on the roof tops – the unfairness of war at its extreme. Such stories go on and on and one could get totally immersed in sorrow but on that day, what a day it was, hope and life started again.

The Army Leclerc stayed in central Paris only two days because they had to pursue the Germans and there was quite a bit of fighting going on in some suburbs. Then the Americans arrived. They came in waves of tanks and trucks full of soldiers and Paris was exploding with joy – Glen Miller played all night, having been installed in Place de la Concorde, and everybody danced and danced. Even when some desperate snipers went on shooting, people went on dancing; then the snipers were discovered one after another and shot on the spot. This is part of my life I will certainly never forget.

PARIS – AFTER AUGUST, 1944

Happy and yet very anxious. The joy of being free was immense but now came the wait to see who had made it through those awful years. The sadness at the loss of friends once so cherished and now gone was tremendous and the impatience one felt for the ones we knew nothing about was indescribable but we all pulled through, with the various tragedies and the memories of good times past. The reuniting of families brought with it such a feeling of relief; in some cases people had not seen or heard of one another for four years or so. Imagine the sense of relief to know that someone was actually alive after such a long silence. The war was over for Paris but not for the rest of Europe.

However, there was one very sad, unpleasant and long-lasting sequel to all this: France had been terribly deeply divided; families and friendships and loyalties of all sorts had been split down the middle and this had given rise to unprecedented internecine hatreds. There were those French men and women who were uncompromisingly determined to expel the Germans from France and quite prepared to die for their convictions. There were those who were prepared to cooperate with the Germans – for whatever reason, be it fear of communism, admiration of orderliness however crude, acceptance of skilful propaganda, anti-Semitism, fundamental and historic dislike for and resentment of the successes of the Anglo-Saxons, or the most depraved form of profit making by denunciation for money which did such tragic damage to the Resistance. The attitude of the French police was unpredictable and varied from place to place. Some were very good and helped the

Resistance and some, especially in the unoccupied part of France, were even worse than the Gestapo, in particular in arresting Jews.

However, it was then that the first American, Canadian and English soldiers came to Paris on leave. Paris had to accommodate these valiant soldiers and officers' clubs were formed to distract them from their duties and from being out in the field. Different clubs were set up for the different nationalities. The Rainbow Corner on Boulevard des Italiens was for the Americans and, across the street, was another for the Canadians and there were several more. The Canadian Officers' Club was organized by a friend of my mother's. She asked my mother whether I would be allowed to go from time to time in the early evening to chat and dance with these Canadian officers, to entertain them a bit, seeing that I spoke some English.

I listened to this conversation from behind the door and my mother asked her friend for assurance that only Canadian and no British officers would come there because, while she was sure that I would not get involved with a Canadian as Canada was so far away, she would not wish me to meet and perhaps get interested in a Brit. I was furious and refused to have anything to do with the idea, even though it would have been an opportunity to dance. However, some days later my friend Solange phoned me and said: " We absolutely have to go and try out the Canadian Club. From what I have been told, it is incredible; there is hot water and real soap in the cloakrooms and they hand out champagne flutes and chocolate éclairs, as many as you like. It is sensational. Also, there is central heating and you do not even need a cardigan". Well, this was it. You must remember these luxuries had been so lacking during the war that very little got us excited and this was the cave of Alibaba as far as we were concerned. I was just 19 and I could not believe my ears.

At this time I was studying history of art at l'Ecole du Louvre. I thoroughly enjoyed the class and spent a lot of time there. After class, early one evening, my friend and I decided to go to the Canadian Club together. We should have been met and chaperoned by my mother's friend, but she was ill with 'flu and thus not available to introduce us. You see, it was customary to be introduced to the officers; after all, we were respectable young ladies. Feeling many pairs of eyes on us and somewhat intimidated, my friend said under her breath " Let's knock back some bubbly and consume our éclairs and then we will see...." So we sat ourselves down at one of the tables overlooking the dance floor and started our feast, delighted that we had got this far without any problem. "I bet you don't have the nerve to go and introduce yourself to those officers" said my friend. Sitting at another table not far from us were two British officers who were chatting and looking in our direction. My friend and I had been very aware of them but had not devised a plan of getting to talk to them until my friend came up with a bet that I would not dare to go and talk to them.

"Well, that all depends how much this bet is worth" I said.

"50 francs" was the answer. This was a lot of money back then. So I got up and went towards their table. Once there, I introduced myself and told them of the bet. This broke the ice and we were naturally invited to join them. I was intrigued by them specially because, as they were in battle dress, they were surely on leave from somewhere in Normandy, and, as we had had a family house in that region for the last three generations and as there had been lots of destruction, mining, bombing and fighting there, we were wondering if our house was still standing.

On the Eiffel Tower, October 1944

There was a great band playing some Glen Miller dance music and the dance floor was very inviting. After chatting a bit, one of the officers asked me for a dance. Whilst dancing I asked him where he had come from in Normandy. He answered that he could not tell me as the fighting was still going on, so I said: " I am only asking you this because I know Normandy really well; my parents have a house there and maybe you know the place, so describe to me where you are and maybe I will guess it''. So he did and I eventually said: "The place is Houlgate, the street is Avenue du Sporting, the name of the house where you sleep is "Beauregard" and your headquarters is "Le Castel" He was dumbfounded. Well, I was correct and they could not believe their ears and neither could my friend nor I. This was the beginning of a most enjoyable evening. We then realised that, like two Cinderellas, we had to leave to catch the last Metro. We naturally wanted to see each other again and realising they only had 48 hours leave, we hastily made arrangements to meet again the next day. I wanted my parents to have news of our home and I was in a whirl of excitement beyond description about the whole situation. So I invited them for lunch the next day.

When I told my parents at breakfast that I had invited two British officers to lunch that day they were furious. There was hardly any food in the house and the pantry was bare. I told them that it really did not matter but the important thing was to be able to have news and to forget the etiquette of hospitality. I explained what had happened at the Canadian Officers' Club and how I had pinpointed the officers' location.

The door bell rang and there was one officer – the one whose name was Guy – like a father Christmas bringing chocolates, soap, and tinned food. He spoke French well but with a terrible accent and my father and he were off on long discussions about the whole encounter because another strange twist was the fact we met in the Canadian Club, whereas Guy and his companion were British. There actually were very few Brits about. Why Houlgate? Why those particular houses? Destiny was looming in there somewhere and I had no idea where all this was going to lead.

Lunch finished late and Guy had to leave to get back to Normandy and get on with the war. He was in the Royal Signals and was then in charge of restoring communications first in the beach-head area and then on through northern France, Belgium, Holland and into Germany. This entailed repairing broken and laying new telegraph and telephone lines in areas which had been fought through, so Guy was in the perfect place for staying in touch with us, as he was often be able to get through on the engineering circuits of the telephone system as it was gradually restored. Little did I realise that this was the beginning of a telephone friendship which would soon turn into a telephone romance. I believe that nowadays the internet would be the equivalent! He would call from time to time. Each time they moved on and established a new headquarters he would call, sometimes at two in the morning so as not to take the lines at times when they were needed for important traffic. The test clerks in the French telephone exchanges were most understanding and helpful and, when Guy made these calls, their response was always: "Bonsoir mon Capitaine. Je suis tout à fait au courant. Attendez un instant" and the call would be put through. Needless to say, my parents were not amused by these nocturnal conversations. As the telephone bell was so loud and the corridor so long before you reached the telephone, the noise made in order to answer the telephone woke everyone up. The floor boards under the carpet had needed fixing ever since before the war and the creaks and squeaks were quite musical but not to the joy of the elders.

Time passed, the calls went on for a year and came from northern France, then from Belgium, then from Holland and finally from Germany. I followed the war via telephone and visualized the pushing back of the Germans. I tried to understand my interest in this officer – though I really had not seen much of him but was beginning to know him by telephone – not the usual romantic encounter.

Then in one call, a year and a half since the last time I saw him, Guy told me that he had some fifteen days leave coming in July and could we see each other. I agreed and immediately set about trying to arrange a plan for this time. I asked my cousin by marriage, Nicole Bréguet who had a house in Antibes in the South of France and whom I had introduced to her husband when we were in Megève, if I could come to stay during the month of July and told her about this officer who was showing great interest in me although we hardly knew each other, other than by voice on the telephone. I mentioned his leave and the opportunity this would give me to get to know this voice better. She accepted immediately because she owed me a favour for having made it possible for her to meet another cousin of mine, Pierre Bréguet, with whom she fell madly in love and subsequently married, as mentioned previously. She had also just given birth to their second child, a daughter whose godmother I was, and I could help out with the baby during my stay. This must have seemed totally acceptable to my parents because they let me go and they knew that another female cousin, Christiane de la Bruyère, would be there also.

So, after the long absence, I found myself in the company of the Royal Signals officer whose voice I knew, it was strange to start all over again to get to know this individual who was later to change my life totally. The Riviera was at its best. The weather was flawless during his whole leave and the oleanders decorating the countryside were abundant in their colour and splendour. Now at this period all the best night clubs and casinos along the coast were reserved for the American troops. Seeing how much I loved to dance, it was imperative to get in to these places, as all the best jazz orchestras were playing – an opportunity not to be missed – and there were also the fabulous restaurants. Thanks to Guy and to the friendliness of his American comrades-in-arms, we were allowed in and my cousin, who was a very good-looking tall blonde, was always such a hit that we ended up having a great time wherever we went. My cousin's success made it all the more hilarious.

At this time, Pierre Bréguet, my cousin's husband, had the use of a six-metre yacht "Namoussa" moored in the Bay of Cannes. It belonged to his father, Louis Bréguet, and with it came a sailor, inevitably called Marius, who looked after the boat and maintained it superbly. Pierre very kindly lent us the boat for several days. You can imagine the envy of the Americans, seeing the only British officer along the Riviera at that time alone on board with three women and the "crew", having a wonderful time. The Americans had a bad reputation due the misconduct of a few of them, so many women refused to go out with them, though I am sure there were plenty of decent men there. However, there were many stories of rape and kidnapping; some of these soldiers just did not know how to behave, which ruined the enjoyment for the well-deserving others, who just wanted to go and have a good time. That said, we had tremendous fun under the benevolent if watchful eyes of some envious American officers.

At the end of fifteen days of paradise, my British officer had to leave to report back to duty in Nienburg an der Weser. I now knew him better and realised that he was intelligent and independent-minded with great qualities – an individual far removed from the people I was brought up with and with whom I expected to continue living. I had been exposed through Guy to a completely different way of thinking, had realised that he refused to accept conventional wisdom on any subject without testing it logically to his own satisfaction and, due to all the hardships and sorrows of the war, I was eager for change and probably very receptive to this kind of thinking. Some of his ideals I was not in agreement with but it was so refreshing to have another perspective. The French bourgeoisie was so different from the English one which, historically, was so much freer and, for the French, hard to understand.

It was only much later that I realised that, under the surface of this apparently rather serious individual, was a highly-developed sense of the ridiculous which could usually take the stress out of life's inevitable disagreements. Guy had been brought up in England by his mother, Alice, who had divorced her Swedish husband when Guy was two. She had always lived in

England but went to school in Belgium and spoke French quite well. Guy went through English schooling, ending up a typical product of British education, with the ideals of being ever faithful to Crown and country. He had a sheltered and somewhat sickly childhood but was adored by his mother, whose third and only surviving child he was, and who watched over him intensely and relentlessly. (The first was still-born and the second died of Seliac disease aged two.) He did not have much freedom then, but his mother, to the best of her limited material ability, had taken him travelling around Western Europe to give him as wide a knowledge as she could. He stayed with families in Germany in the summer holidays when he was 15 and 16 to improve his school German. At 17, to his, his mother's and his school's terrible disappointment, he was articled to a London solicitor (then the first step in one sort of legal training). This was at the insistence of Alice's two brothers, on whom she was partly financially dependent, who did not understand the value of university education. It was also particularly exasperating because Guy's education was not costing anyone very much; he had a scholarship at his school and everyone seemed confident that he would get another one to a university.

The next year, 1938, Guy reckoned that war was inevitable and joined the Territorial Army. On the outbreak of war he was called up aged 19 and a little later he was sent on an eight month course at the Royal Signals Officer Cadet Training Unit and then commissioned. He served for almost exactly seven years, ending up a major.

Having learnt all about his past and now that he was gone again, I realised that I did have feelings for him and that I had fallen in love with him. I was now confronted with the task of letting this fact be known to my parents. What was their reaction going to be that their only daughter had fallen in love with a British officer?

Upon my return from the South of France I had to tell my parents that the British officer who had been bombarding me with those phone calls for the last year, had come to join us in Antibes, that I had fallen in love with him and that I wanted to go to England for his next leave to meet his mother. My father was quite in favour but my mother was violently opposed. I was ready to fight it.

CHRISTMAS AND MARRIAGE – 1945 AND 1946

It was November when Guy told me that he had some confirmed leave that December. He wanted to return to England to see his mother, whom he had not seen since just before the Normandy landing in 1944 and who, he knew from her doctor, was suffering from cancer. He was very anxious to introduce me to her and therefore was insistent that I joined him there. We had talked about a possible trip to England at Christmas whilst in the South of France that past July and, ever since my return, I had looked into the possibility of travelling.

Travel between England and the Continent was then extremely restricted and one needed all sorts of papers for permission to travel, and civilians at that time were not normally allowed to. One had to submit a very detailed visa application stating exactly the reason for travel and it was a long-winded procedure. The first time I presented myself to the British Consulate in Paris, having queued for three hours, I was asked the purpose of my trip. I innocently replied that I was going to visit the mother of a British officer whom I had met and that I was joining him on his leave there. The bureaucrat across the table put down his pen, peered over his half moon glasses and burst out laughing saying that I could not be serious and that the reason was not acceptable. It would be so easy for every young French woman who had met an Englishman to apply for a visa and go to England. One had to have a valid, working reason in order to obtain a visa.

So, unperturbed, I went and sought counsel with uncle Louis Bréguet, to whom I referred above, who at that time was travelling on business a lot between England and France and told him the whole story so far. He told me not to worry, that he would write a letter explaining that I was his secretary and that he needed me to travel to England and it was imperative for his business. So, armed with this letter and appropriate documents, I stood in line for another three hours only to fall on the same man. He looked at me, he looked at the letter and then at the documents, then spun around again on his office chair to face and open a drawer in his filing cabinet only to turn around to say: "You were already here three days ago with a totally different reason than this for your trip. This therefore is a fake" and he tore everything up in front of me. He explained that the only viable purpose to go to England would be to be married. I could not believe my ears. What was I to do?

I was expecting a call from Guy who at that time was in Nienburg and would be calling to find out whether all the paper work had been done for the coming trip. So when the telephone rang and I told him what had happened he responded by saying straight away; "Well, let's get married then". Not quite the proposal that I had envisaged and now, when I think back, what an unromantic proposal it was. Did he actually ever ask me to marry him (he always says he didn't)? I then told him I had to figure something out to tell my parents and that he had to wait a little longer before a final decision could be made.

How was I going to announce this to my parents? I did not sleep a wink that night. There I was, twenty years old, still young and on the brink of throwing myself on some roller coaster. The telephone calls grew more frequent as Guy wanted to know the decision. Finally by phone I said: "C'est d'accord but let's not breathe a word to my parents because if they know the real reason for me to go to England they will never agree".

Once again, with a letter from Guy stating the real reason for my trip, I went to the consulate. I waited another three hours, showed the letter saying that Guy absolutely wanted me to join him in England as we were to be married. The paper-work was taken away and a wait of another half hour ended with a visa being stamped into my French passport. The stamp read "valid single journey only for marriage".

I returned home and told my parents that I had finally got my visa but I made a point of not showing it to them and started on further arrangements. Inside I was very troubled about not telling them the whole deal. I was their only daughter and a wedding in the church would be their idea of how things were properly done. I did not dare tell a soul, not even my best friend Solange, for fear of the cat being let out of the bag. I wanted no-one to know that I had embarked on an adventure that was only just beginning and I wanted no-one to know the truth as to why I was going to England.

At that time Protestantism in France was still very strict; the Protestants remained amongst themselves and often did not mix with the Catholics. My family was Protestant and I had been brought up in that religion. Guy was a tolerant agnostic – at least he was not a Roman Catholic – which would have been totally unacceptable to my parents. We had a delightful pastor whom I liked a lot. During the war he held all us youngsters together and kept us going with hope and had an incredible aura about him that made him very special to us all. I suddenly realised that I could unload my story on him and feel some sort of relief. He was the only person on whom I could rely for his silence and forgiveness for this imminent journey to England. I told him everything and what I thought could possibly happen: that I would probably have to have a civil wedding for visa purposes in England but, that after, I would be free to return and have a proper Protestant wedding at his church, where I hoped he would marry us the next time Guy was on leave. Knowing me well and trusting me, he agreed. The relief for me was immense and the knowledge that my parents would have the religious wedding, which they would consider necessary and appropriate, was comforting, seeing that without that assurance they would have been quite beside themselves.

I left for England on December 19th 1945 by train. This train was packed full of military personnel and I counted only four civilians in all. This was the beginning of an adventure which I shall never forget. The smell of cigarettes, the mumble of the English language and the occasional outburst of laughter as the train was making its way through northern France towards Calais will remain an impression well ground into my memory...what was I embarking on? The train rattled its way through the bare wintry landscape and finally reached Calais where we boarded a ship bound for England that afternoon. The ship was as full as the train, loads of people and bustling. The sea was extremely rough, so the crossing was awful. One imagined the ship being a cork bobbing up and down uncontrollably on the wild waves. I watched and felt numb. People around me rushing out on deck to breathe the sea air or be sick, the air inside was bad and sour-smelling from the vomit of those who had not found their sea-legs. Then I became excited and nervous at the same time as we approached Dover.

We disembarked, then it was Immigration, which was conducted by the military. I was beginning to come to terms with queuing for the English after my numerous hours waiting for my visa at the consulate in Paris. This seemed ridiculous after such a crossing but at last it was my turn. All of a sudden everything started to slow down even more, my passport was taken away, then I was led off for a medical examination, only to come out of that to be interrogated about my trip. The interrogators even telephoned Guy's headquarters in Nienburg to find out whether my story was true. In those days you did not just pick up a telephone and dial a number; you placed a call and awaited the connection. Time seemed to have stopped. Then I was asked many more questions. One has to remember the war had just ended and Britain, expecting an onslaught of refugees, had to protect itself against an infiltration of undesirables and therefore made entry into the country as difficult as possible. Of course with all this delay I missed the train going to London where Guy's mother and his RAF cousin, John Raper, were awaiting my arrival. I had to wait another two hours and was accompanied throughout by a soldier who was kind and polite and insisted on carrying my luggage. I was terrified, my English was not good but I understood pretty much everything. My main concern was how to get word to the people expecting me.

Luckily the Immigration officers were kind enough to get a message through to London where a loud speaker informed my pick-up party of my unavoidable delay. The train pulled into Victoria station and I stepped out on to a crowded platform, dressed in the clothes I said I would be wearing and carrying a Figaro so that my future mother-in-law could recognize me. I spotted immediately a very handsome RAF officer – Guy's cousin John Raper – and an old lady looking pale and tired. My relief was immediate: I had found them. For them it was easy to find me, as there were hardly any civilians in the train and I was accompanied by my military escort.

It was then that I was told that Guy would not be back from Nienburg until the following day. Well, you can imagine how alone I felt in England, which is so drastically different from France. The first of many immediate gut feelings emerged and I awaited Guy's return with impatience.

After having spent the first few days with my fiancé and his mother, being presented to family and friends, I had to start to arrange my return. I had no passport any more as at Immigration they had said: "seeing that you are coming to get married, from now on you will have a British passport" and that was the last I saw of my French passport. So the first thing to do was to get married at the Registry Office. I told Guy that I wanted to start the procedures after Christmas as I did not want to spoil my parents' Christmas. As I was not yet twenty-one I needed their consent to be married. So after Christmas I telephoned my parents and broke the news to them that I had no more French passport, that I had to get a British passport because my French one served as a one way ticket and therefore, in order to return, I needed to get married at the Registry Office for the formalities and that we would have a proper wedding in April in Paris, but I needed their consent. I need not tell you more but you can imagine how this very bourgeois French couple had just been smacked in the face with a preposterous ultimatum about which they could do absolutely nothing. After twenty-four hours digesting their daughter's news, they consented to the marriage and sent a telegram to that effect. Knowing that a religious ceremony was in line for them made it all acceptable. The following ten days of Guy's leave were spent touring southern England, with petrol coupons enabling us to travel, and ended with the Registry Office marriage.

Once we went to have dinner with one of Guy's oldest friends. It was extremely foggy on our way home, I had at one stage to walk along the road with a torch to show Guy the way. Then we got totally lost and it was near St. Albans that we went into a police station, where Guy caused mirth by asking for a cell to spend the night in. However, they were not allowed to accommodate a woman. So they rang up a hospital and at 2 a.m. we arrived there and they gave us a whole ward to ourselves. It was an empty former war casualty ward. The astonishment of the nurses when they saw us in the early morning, especially Guy's uniform on a hanger and me in the next bed, was quite fun to see.

On 29th December 1945 we were married in the Registry Office in Slough. We were alone, with Guy's mother and one of her friends, Betsan Harrison, as witnesses, and that was it.... I really did not have the feeling of being married nor did I feel any real jubilation. It was all rather flat but this somewhat icy situation was warmed by the fact that the Registrar, who explained that he had just been demobilized himself, kept on getting the procedure for the ceremony wrong and we had to go back to the beginning. Then, to add to that, at the point where one has to repeat some words after the Registrar, I got it wrong and instead of saying "my lawful wedded husband" I blurted out "my awful wedded husband". After that everyone burst out laughing and there really was nothing decorous or emotional about the ceremony at all. An element of sadness lingered inside me and I hoped that the religious wedding would be heart-warming and more memorable.

Once married I could now start the procedure to get a British passport. Bureaucracy is notorious for being slow so, with that plus total disorganization due to the war, it was going to take six weeks to get the passport and before I could leave for France again. Guy's leave came to an end a few days after the marriage and it was time for him to return to his HQ. So there I was stuck in England, living with my mother-in-law 30 minutes from London. I was taken care of very well. England was still rationed both for food and clothing, and people, upon hearing that I had come from France, were generous and gave me whatever coupons they could spare. All our war suffering under the German occupation had been reported in England and it seemed that everyone was aware of the hardship we had gone through and it was heart-warming to be cared for in that way.

When the passport came through and I was allowed to return, I was very aware of how sick my mother-in-law was with head and stomach aches, and upon setting foot in France I wondered whether I would ever see her again. I did not. She died the 12th of April, 1946, the day after our Paris wedding, of generalized cancer.

My parents organised the wedding and we went to Paris and naturally stayed at their flat. On the morning of the great day, my father shocked Guy by saying: "Mon vieux, tu me fais un grand service: ma fille a un caractère de cochon" (Old boy you're doing me a great favour: my daughter is impossible.) Guy felt – and has always felt since – that it was unpleasant and not entirely in jest. I suppose my presence tended to get in the way of the social life which was always so dear to my parents. We were married again in Paris at l'Eglise Reformée de l'Etoile the 11th April 1946 and it was a beautiful spring day. The church was full to burst; it was the curiosity of seeing a local girl marrying a British Officer. It was, in fact, a very small wedding and only about one quarter of the people in the church had been invited to the reception. There was a moment of shock in the vestry where we went to sign the book, because the parson said that the civil marriage had already taken place in England on the 29th December 1945. Such a thing was unheard of because, normally, it would have taken place that same morning. There was lots of whispers, laughing and other noises. Poor Guy knew three people in all the congregation; it took a long time and was a real ordeal for him. As we emerged into the bright sunlight outside the church, Frank Hooper, the best man, a colleague of Guy's from his HQ, was heard, above the general noise of conversation, to say: "For Christ's sake smile".

Wedding 11th April 1946, Paris

The bubbles barely popped in the blood stream and the day after our wedding my husband left me to go to England to make the funeral arrangements for his mother. I, on the other hand, returned to my parents' flat as if nothing had happened and Guy returned to Germany after England. I did not see him again until July, when he was demobilized. Nobody could understand; my friends remembered coming to my wedding on the 11th and on the 12th I was back home with my parents and was then seen being taken out by Frank, the best man, who was trying to cheer me up. What was going on?

July finally came, I returned to England and we settled down in the small house in Gerrards Cross, Buckinghamshire, which Alice had built for herself and Guy when her marriage broke up. She had also accommodated in it, in turn, her mother and her father in their last illnesses and later a spinster cousin, a retired school-teacher about 10 years older than Alice and universally known as Aunt Blanche. Aunt Blanche lived with Alice from 1932 until Alice's death. For years it worked satisfactorily but Aunt Blanche grew more and more difficult and the prospect for a newly married couple to have to look after her was daunting, to say the least. However a totally unexpected salvation was at hand. A splendid, rumbustious cousin of Alice's, named Tina Midgley, married with grown-up children, said: "Alice has carried this burden for long enough and I will not allow it be imposed on Guy and his new young wife". So Aunt Blanche was removed, protesting violently, to Tina's house in Northwood, where she spent her last few years in comfort. Then we reminded ourselves that a honeymoon was due. Finally, too, we were together. So getting into Guy's old pre-war Standard 8 (Guy had carefully put it on blocks in the garage in 1941 "just in case I survive this war") we set off on our honeymoon to Switzerland. This car was far from new but it was a privilege to have one at all as not many people could travel and the freedom was incredible. This car was not water-tight and every time it rained I had to hold up a coat or, better still, open up an umbrella inside, to divert the deluge from the skies away from us inside. When we crossed the Franco-Swiss frontier at Les Verrières, the Swiss customs impounded our two precious 2-gallon tins of petrol which made us furious. To our surprise, we recovered them a month later, on the way back, but to do so were obliged to leave Switzerland at the same frontier post. We went to a little hotel in Les Verrières for dinner and the night and had to warn the patronne that we had no Swiss currency and would not be able to pay until we had changed some tourist coupons at the bank. She said there was no bank in the village but she would trust us to send her the amount by post. That cheered us up, after having our spare petrol impounded.

My mother-in-law in her will had asked to be cremated and then to have her ashes scattered on a mountain top. Guy decided to carry out the request and so off we drove, with the ashes in the boot, to the Swiss Alps – a trip which would be done many times years later, sometimes with our children, and sometimes without. We had decided that we would go walking in the Alps and so the ashes were stored in a box, which we then could put in a backpack and easily carry up a mountain.

We had been lent, for part of our stay, a beautiful chalet belonging to a friend of Guy's uncle. It was perched on a mountain side overlooking the Wallensee, with a spectacular view. This was to be the beginning of our honeymoon. After getting there and scouting out the area for several days, we decided on which mountain to scatter the ashes. Off we went early one morning to climb the chosen mountain, the Säntis, walking through fields of wild flowers and hearing distant cow bells ringing and not actually seeing the cows. It was a warm sunny day. The climb up took up the better part of the morning and we finally got to the top to be greeted with a superb panoramic view of the mountains about us. The weather was calm and one could hear one's heart pounding recovering from the morning's effort. Guy then decided to open the box and scatter the ashes. Just as he did this, there was a tremendous gust of wind coming out of nowhere which funnelled up the ashes which then dispersed into the abyss around us. It all happened very fast and was quite strange and uncomfortable for a while. The wind ceased as fast as it came and the clocks ticked forward as if nothing had happened. The experience has always remained with me to this day. I have never really questioned it but feel that it was Alice's last good-bye to her son.

After staying a few more days, we travelled on to Ascona on Lago Maggiore, where we met the conductor Harry Blech and his wife in a charming hotel facing the Lake. Guy earned some Swiss francs, which were a very welcome addition to the then small official allowance, by translating some technical German for a refugee German engineer who owned some patents which were used in German submarines and American Mack trucks. Later on we and the Blechs became great friends and Guy became the treasurer of the Haydn Mozart Society and Harry was the conductor of the London Mozart Players for many years. It was through him that we went to listen to many concerts at the Festival Hall and, as treasurer, Guy had to try to fill it to make the concerts pay.

Then came the return journey via Lausanne to visit some of my relatives. My family being half Swiss, I had cousins scattered all over the place, so we called on many to present Guy. The Vaud canton of Switzerland which we were visiting is famous for its cheese and chocolate, so we made sure to stock up on these before returning to England where our life was to take another turn.

END OF CONFLICT AND ENGLAND - 1946 - 54

Once back in England we had to face the consequences of Guy's decision not to stay in the Army. As the time for Guy's demobilization approached he had been faced with a huge dilemma: he had been a successful officer in the Royal Signals during the War, both as a regimental and a staff officer, and was pressed by his Chief Signal Officer to apply for a regular commission – which, in theory, would have secured a career until retiring age – while, on the other hand, he felt that seven years full-time soldiering was, in all respects, enough. The army was being reduced in size; how long he would be able to keep his rank of Temporary Major was uncertain; he was not too keen on the idea of peace-time soldiering; he did not think that I would readily take to being a British Army wife. Which I certainly would not have liked one bit.

So he decided not to apply for a regular commission and to face the alternative of a return to student status at the age of 26, to qualify as a solicitor (having got half-way there before the war) and find a job in something other than private practice of the law – which he knew he loathed – in which his legal training would be an advantage. After much thought and discussion, he got to work to pass the Solicitors' Final examination, with the help of a tiny government grant for ex-officers, passed it and then got a job as Assistant Secretary of the Colonial Development Corporation, which was a body set up to invest public money in colonial projects of a type which would not be profitable enough to attract private investors. Having established that he still was capable, after 7 years interruption, of studying a subject which he hated, Guy reckoned he ought to be able also to study subjects which interested him. He set about getting an external degree from London University, which, he decided, would be an essential qualification if he was ever to achieve his aim of getting into Public Service. At the same time, in view of the worsening of the world political situation, he joined the Army Emergency Reserve of Officers for several more years of part-time soldiering. This all meant that life was hard for us and I had just given birth to Nicholas, our first son. Guy needed quiet to study when he got home in the evening after his day's work and having a new-born under the same roof as a student was not the happiest time for any of us. I was a new mother without help in a new land with weird habits and my husband was not around much. Returning to Guy's job, he met three people worth mentioning in the CDC: his boss, Sinclair Hunter, the secretary, who taught him a lot, including the maddening accuracy which pervades everything he writes, Hugh Shillito, the corporation's in-house solicitor, and the first Lord Trefgarne, the chairman, whom Guy has often described as the biggest shit he has ever met. After two years of discontent, Guy was fired by Lord Trefgarne for refusing to sign a cheque to pay, with corporation money, for the chairman's wife to join him on holiday in Cyprus.

At that time Hugh Shillito, whom Guy considers as the best friend a man could possibly have, had just left the Corporation, on his own terms, to buy a small city practice (which was the way things worked in those days) from the executors of an old solicitor who had just died. Hugh telephoned Guy and offered him a job: to help him sort out the muddle that this practice had fallen into and offered Guy a grand total of six pounds a week. This was a blessing and Guy accepted gratefully.

Guy carried on working for his degree. He worked extremely hard, for three years, at Latin, German and French. He worked every evening into the early hours and all of either Saturday or Sunday. In the middle of all this, Shillito offered him a partnership (unheard of in those days, without paying for it) which Guy, after much thought, turned down with many thanks, saying he would rather continue as a paid hand until he could get what he wanted – whatever that might turn out to be.

Eventually Guy took and passed the Foreign (later re-named Diplomatic) Service entrance examination, but there was a nine-month delay while I and my parents were investigated to make sure that we were neither communists nor fascists and had not done anything against British interests during or since the War. That started him off on 35 years service, along with which I went for the ride, and we shared a host of experiences of all sorts some of which will be related later in this book. I, in the meantime, had given birth to Jeremy, our second child, and had my hands full with two small children. We had a succession of young continental girls who came to improve their English and help me out. One of them, Lily Tschuppert, later Fischer, from Luzern, has remained a dear friend ever since, and we often see her during our visits to Switzerland.

My feelings for this new career were very mixed. I had no idea what it would be like; I looked forward to the travel which, I presumed, would be involved. I could not help wondering whether we would be able to make a success of it. However, having been through the four terrible years of the Nazi occupation of France, I was ready for anything.

After about two years in London, Guy was given his first foreign posting, to Berlin. Nick was 6 and Jeremy 2 ½.

I do not propose to embark on yet another history of the Cold War. The reader either knows it, to a greater or less degree, or should read it in the works of people better informed about it than I. Suffice it to say that, in a bitterly divided world, the Soviet Union was trying to become supreme everywhere by a policy of unlimited, utterly unscrupulous, dishonest and treacherous aggression under the guise of "communism" and the West was frantically trying to prevent it. In addition to defending the countries already committed to freedom and democracy, this entailed trying to open the eyes of the uncommitted neutrals to what the Soviets were really up to. In Berlin and Vienna the two sides faced each other openly. In April 1949 NATO had been set up with the intention of effectively restraining Soviet military power. Each member country contributed people and money for mutual defence. The example of Hitler and his doings had proved that only a tightly united defence pact would deter another potential aggressor from misbehaving. After various scares and vicissitudes (e.g. the Berlin blockade and airlift, the Bay of Pigs, the reunification of Germany and the disintegration of Yugoslavia and the USSR) NATO has, thank God, shown that it is still very much alive.

BERLIN - 1954-56

It was one evening early in August 1954 when Guy returned from work that he announced his first posting. At last a posting and we could leave for something new; it was finally going to start happening – whatever it was. Much had to be done in order to leave home for Germany: house to pack up and let and – most important – I had to pass my driving test. Guy left in September, leaving me to finish off the last of the packing and I found myself alone doing the finishing touches of clearing the house which had not been done since Alice had it built in 1922.

Tenants were found through an advertisement in the Times newspaper. The boys were sent to their grand parents in Paris and I had the last load of Guy's books to put up in the loft. The following day was my driving test and then I was to go to Paris to pick up the boys and take them to Berlin. I had to carry the books, in groups of twelve stacked high, and climb a ladder, perch the books on the edge of the trap door then jump up into the loft to put the books in cases up there. The loft was not floored so, to add to everything else, I had to balance on the joists. Quite a balancing act and, as night fell, it had to be done in the light of a candle as there was no electricity up there. It was the last load and, with the books neatly packed in the cases, I stepped back to admire the organised chaos of the loft, slipped between the joists and fell crashing through the ceiling, landing, luckily, on the top tier of my son's book case in the room below and not down the stair well. However, in the fall my left arm was stuck in the loft, so I was sitting there with one arm up and one arm down as if directing traffic. No one was in the house with me and through some misschance the candle blew out so that in my graceful fall the only light I had was the shine from a street lamp outside. My charred remains would have looked most peculiar in my then posture had the house gone up in flames. Slowly but surely, I wriggled and writhed out of my position, in pain. I thought I had broken my wrist, and at one in the morning found myself finally disentangled. The next day I saw the doctor and explained that I had to pass my driving test and that he had to bind up my wrist very tight and drug me up. So, dosed up, I went for my test and passed – I often think it was because I had a super quick reaction in slamming on the brakes and not killing a child who ran out after a ball in front of the car. Now it was off to France.

Once in Paris, I retrieved my sons and we left for Berlin by train via Frankfurt am Main. Nick was in a fine mess, he had a stinking cold, red eyes and was coughing and Jeremy had pigged out on chocolate cake. He proceeded to be sick the whole trip between Paris and Frankfurt. Once in Frankfurt, we recovered a little in a hotel for the night and the next day we were put in a comfortable compartment in the American military train heading for Berlin. This train was transporting a whole American regiment so we were lucky to have our compartment. My sons were feeling a little better and were entertained by the soldiers for most of the twelve hour trip, playing games and cards.

The train crossed the border from the American zone into the Russian zone, in which we remained until Berlin. It seemed to take forever; what with the controls, stopping and starting, it was exasperating. I looked out of the window to see farmers using horses and carts and no machinery. It was squalid and amazing to see how stuck in time they were, as if from another era.

Guy was waiting for us at the station. We got off the train feeling terrible and the boys were definitely not well. We got to the flat which was to be our new home and what a disaster that was. A modern, convenient and totally characterless environment. I looked over to Nick and saw that he was covered in spots. Upon entering the apartment his measles spots had erupted – I suddenly wondered how many of the poor Americans would go down with this, maybe the whole regiment. They certainly would remember their journey! So, that was the beginning of Berlin.

Guy left us shortly afterwards to go to work. There I was alone in this sterile place with two sick sons. This would not do. We were in a block of flats in Charlottenburg Platz, near the NAAFI (Navy, Army and Airforce Institute) and the British Officers' Club and close to Guy's office at the Olympic Stadium, where the army and the military government had their offices, but it was awful.

It did not take me long to find a large house with a garden in Grunewald. It had once been the Czech consul's home, which had then become a Gestapo office. No one wanted to live there as it was reputed to be haunted by the ghosts of the victims of Gestapo torture, and apparently the basement had housed prisoners of whom many never saw the light of day again. But it was a fabulous house which would do us fine and we never saw any of the ghosts. I realised this was a large undertaking but I was going to be creative about running this house. We found two Berlin students to live in the coach house/garage who, in return for lodging, stoked the central heating and helped out during official parties by serving, bar-tendering and so on. The house turned out to be great for all purposes and one of the students gave me German lessons. This was not one of my favourite languages and after the war was not high in my priorities. However, I was living in Germany and I needed to be able to communicate somehow.

Our Berlin House, 1954

The English school was not much good, so Nick, being bilingual, went to the French Lycée which was, of course, in the French sector. So as to reduce the number of car journeys, I formed a car pool with three other British families who also had bilingual children. Slowly we were getting settled. Through the school I met some

French wives of French officers and a bartering system developed; one bottle of whisky was worth twelve of red wine, so we joined in enjoying every drop of vino as we could easily procure whisky through the NAAFI. One must remember that Berlin was an island within the Soviet Zone and we lived as if by rationing: availability of small luxuries was very limited. I had had a good training through the war and was accustomed to these types of exchanges.

The climate was very continental, hot in summer and cold in winter and extremely dry. This unfortunately did Jeremy no good as he was asthmatic. He nearly died of double pneumonia and throughout the winter he never went out for fear of getting sick again. A near death experience with a child in a foreign country is not something I would wish for anyone. To come so close to losing someone and be incapable of communicating is desperately alarming.

Our house turned out to be quite a party house. It lent itself brilliantly to crowds and, with the team of people I had working for us, it was an eventful time. We met many people and unfortunately one of them was the Soviet agent George Blake, who was posted to Berlin during our time there. George Blake was what Guy calls a British object, that is to say someone who had a British passport but no roots in Britain. His father was an Egyptian who had somehow obtained British citizenship and his mother was Dutch. He escaped from Holland to England at the beginning of the WW II, joined the Royal Navy and had an adequate and uneventful war. He was a good linguist and was employed on duties in which his languages were required. On demobilization he slipped easily into what was then called the Foreign Service and in due course was posted to Seoul in Korea as vice-consul. When the Korean war broke out Seoul was overrun and Blake was taken away as a prisoner and handed over to the Russians. Then, as was subsequently revealed after his treachery was discovered, he was recruited by the KGB to work against Britain. At his trial he claimed that his motive was idealistic in that he became convinced that communism was right and western capitalism wicked and wrong but later, in prison, he admitted that his motive was simply that he saw the possibility of greater reward and fame in working for the Russians. So this he did, for several years, and did a great deal of damage to Britain and the USA until caught in 1961, tried for treason and condemned to 42 years in prison. He was sent to Wormwood Scrubs, supposedly the most secure jail in England, but escaped. It later transpired that the Russians, through an Irishman, organised the escape by buying people along the line to make it possible. Moscow acclaimed the arrival of their agent back among them but Blake, having lost access to anything of interest, was now of no use. He then married a Russian, lived quite comfortably in Russia and has shown no sign of shame or regret for his treachery or for causing the death of those whom he betrayed. This has been made abundantly clear by his performance in several TV programs. Guy's relationship with Blake was an example of how deception works at its evil best. The blow to Guy and many other colleagues was devastating.

His first wife, Gillian, was a charming person, the very beautiful daughter of a quite distinguished Army Officer, and they had two boys. At the time of his arrest she was expecting their third child and the whole disaster for both her and her family was quite awful. Luckily, a few years later she remarried and started a new life in Australia with another Englishman. I have lost touch completely with her but understandably so, for we were a part of her life with her treacherous husband and why should she ever want to remember that?

At that time the Berlin Wall was not yet built, and it was possible to make contact with people in the Russian Sector. Berlin was a warren of spies from all sides. This made for an extraordinary life style and many encounters led to information and leads to interesting people from the other side. Everyone was getting information or reading between the lines at cocktail parties or in local newspapers — who was telling the truth and who was telling lies and who was leading whom up the garden path was very, very unclear. It was a period of infiltration from both sides, double and triple agents abounded everywhere and generally the espionage world was humming with activity.

Guy worked in the British Political Adviser's office which was, of course, in the British sector. I was not supposed to go into East Berlin. My French friends, wives of Army officers, were allowed to and even had military cars and drivers at their disposal, so with them I went several times to East Berlin. This was especially advantageous at festive times like Christmas, as everything was so much cheaper there because of the low value of the East German currency. I bought lovely wooden toys, decoration, flowers and so on at a fraction of the price of West Berlin and we still have some of the decorations.

We frequented four or five excellent restaurants among which La Maison de France on the Kurfürstendamm springs to mind. The food was delicious and the ambiance lively and fun; many enjoyable evenings were spent there and interesting people met. The British Officers' Club was quite a scene, too. In the summer the tennis courts were good, the pool a godsend and the restaurant immaculate, with great service. We often hired (in their spare time) some of the staff from there to help us out at our own parties, knowing that they would perform to perfection. They were cheap to hire as they preferred to be paid in cigarettes, coffee and boot polish rather than in money.

Having established that Gerwin Franzen, one of our resident students, was a good dancer, on several occasions when Guy was away I went to some fabulous Berlin night clubs. The scenes were lively and the music played was jazz, nothing but jazz. There was also a little theatre where a company called "Die Stachelschweine" (the hedgehogs) played sketches which took the mickey out of the government and the establishment in general. They were a great success in Berlin and accepted in Hamburg but their humour was not appreciated anywhere else. Gerwin explained this by saying that the defeat in the war had shaken people's confidence in everything so much that they did not enjoy fun being made of the new government, which was, after all, the government set up by the winners of the war and, therefore, must be right. They performed in the Berlin and Saxon dialects which I could not understand but Guy could – up to a point. We often went to classical concerts, sometimes by candle-light in the Charlottenburger Schloss.

The British garrison in Berlin included a cavalry regiment and although they were of course equipped with armoured vehicles, their tradition resulted in their having lots of horses around, but there were not enough men capable of riding them all. When it became known that I loved to ride, I joined a group of women who used to take the horses out for exercise. We would ride these highly-strung, energetic beasts into the Grunewald forest and let them gallop along the hunting alleys and paths. These alleys led out into East Berlin but at the frontier there was a large open space which was a mine-field and somehow the horses knew at that point to jam on the brakes and turn around without being asked to. At first I thought I was going to die, the horse I was on was so strong and I did not know about the mine field, so when I saw the world whizzing passed me at a thousand miles an hour I thought: "that's it, I'm a goner". This same horse regularly turned back just before the field every time I was out on him.

Berlin includes two large lakes where people like to sail in the summer. However, the frontier with East Berlin ran through the middle of one lake and, to make matters worse, if you got too close to the border you would be shot at. During our stay in Berlin there were many incidents of straying boats and deaths due to being in the wrong spot – a strange reminder of hostile military presence.

We stayed in touch with some of the foreigners we met in Berlin and especially with one American whose path we crossed again twenty years later in

Washington: David Chavchavadze, a Georgian prince, who lived in America and worked in the CIA. He sang and played the guitar very well and his then wife used to sing and dance. All very Russian and helped to make our parties very lively occasions.

Among good British colleagues were Madeleine and Ian MacKay, with whom we remained in contact for a long time, until she died of cancer in 1979 and he five years later of a heart attack. Ian was a brilliant linguist and mimic and a very funny man. Once, on a hot summer evening, he and Madeleine went to a party and came home separately, each thinking that the other was already back. Madeleine got home first, found, to her surprise, that Ian wasn't there and went to sleep in a deck-chair in the back garden. Ian duly arrived a bit later and, to his surprise, saw no lights in the house and went to sleep in a deck chair in the front garden. They were still in their respective chairs when the next day dawned. They had two horrible spoilt cats called Rochester and Lady Chatterly. Someone organised a fancy dress party and Ian was to go as a Viking. This required, amongst other things, a grotesque helmet and 3 or 4 colleagues, all good German speakers, went to the then biggest department store in Berlin, the K d W (Kaufhaus des Westerns) to buy a kettle, the specifications of which were that, with the bottom cut out and its spout to the front, it would fit on Ian's head. There ensued much absurd bogus discussion among the colleagues about the choice of kettle, to the totally uncomprehending confusion of the German sales staff.

Winters there were very cold and poor Jeremy remained indoors. One time Nick and I were watching people doing a strange pastime of sliding their cars on the frozen Wannsee and all of a sudden a motor cyclist decided to join in. He ventured too far out and fell through into the freezing water. No one helped him, he just dropped out of life, just like that. A strange incident to jump out at me but it was shocking to notice that no one seemed to care. Ice used to form on some roads, so that one could ice skate in the middle of the road. One of Guy's odder colleagues loved to ski, anywhere, and as soon as any snow fell he could often be seen being pulled along by a jeep. He never wanted to miss a powder day, I guess.

This life was not to last much longer. Guy came home two years to the day after our arrival in Berlin and announced that we were posted to Brussels to replace Tony Milne, who had just been diagnosed as having diabetes and had to go home for treatment. Three weeks later we left Berlin with great regret.

BRUSSELS - 1956-58

In -24° centigrade we left Berlin in a totally over-loaded Ford Zephyr, the contents stacked up and held together on the back seat with Guy's dressing gown cord, (the only thing at hand at the time) and the two boys. Driving along the motorway through Eastern Germany in a biting north wind and feeling at one moment the definite demise of a burst tire, we pulled over to realise that the spare was under everything in the boot. The boot had to be disembowelled and the spare put on. Remember that the weather was particularly cold and the whole situation was very annoying and uncomfortable but the ice was broken – no pun intended – when two loose loo rolls took to the heavens, unravelling their comet-like tails in the wind across the empty fields nearby. The rolls were the last objects from the Berlin house that I had laid my hands on and were the first things out of the car even though it was not at the right stop.

Brussels was a very different scene and, luckily for us, the British Ambassador, Sir George Labouchère, was a charming man and he liked us very much and often invited us to official dinners. I sometimes went on my own if Guy was not available and I had to entertain with the Ambassador, as his wife was frequently ill with terrible migraine. I loved these dinners and parties, I was young and enjoyed this type of social life. I believe that this does not happen as much now and I have to admit to having made the most of it. It was in Brussels that I had the first of a series of passages of arms with the wives of French diplomats, with whom, by and large, I did not get on. Perhaps, like some French naval officers, they think it improper for French girls to marry Englishmen. Anyway, this one asked me what my husband's rank was and I told her: "Second Secretary." She looked down her nose and said: "Second Secretary? First or Second class?" I replied: "Either First or Twelfth Class, but certainly not Second". She stomped off in a speechless huff. We met the Swiss Ambassador, Mr. Jacard, another delightful person, and Guy and I soon became "bouche trous" at his parties. He knew I was part Swiss and therefore the situation seemed quite acceptable. A "bouche trou" is a last-minute dinner guest to replace someone who for some reason cannot make it; Guy and I were always game because Jacard was so nice and his table superb.

It was about one of these dinners at the Swiss Ambassador's that there is a memorable story to tell. There were about twenty guests and I was seated between the Belgian Minister of the Interior and the Swiss First Secretary, a certain Mr. Mossad, whom I had met three months previously, a funny-looking little round man. We had talked about some hobbies and he told me that on holiday he liked to make love. This was so funny, coming from such an ugly and unsexy man. I had told him that I liked to play tennis in the summer and ski in the winter and we chatted about further subjects which I have since forgotten. Anyway, I found myself seated next to him and I remember our conversation as if it had taken place yesterday. The Minister started talking and captured my attention, but in the meantime I was very aware of somebody touching my knee and playing footsie from my left side (in other words from Mr.

Mossad's side): cheeky so-and-so, I thought, and it continued. Then all of a sudden what do I see coming out from under the table: an enormous St. Bernard dog. I burst out laughing and said: "Mr. Mossad, for a half hour now I was under the impression that you were playing footsie with me but I see now this huge dog". He blushed profusely, poor man, and was at a loss for words. But the funniest part was that sitting opposite was the Papal Nuncio, sitting next to Mme. Mossad, who was and looked quite unmistakably English, and said "Well then, Monseigneur, I too for the last twenty minutes thought you were playing footsie with me and now I see the dog". This was uproariously funny because Mme. Mossad looked like a typical prude from a Victorian novel, very shy, small and dressed in pale pink. It brought the house down and in the general mirth which ensued, the waiters had the greatest difficulty in not dropping their dishes containing a magnificent sweet which was a splendid "pièce montée" of profiterolles glazed with caramel, especially when a piece broke off, flew through the air and went down the shirtfront of the Minister of the Interior. The Papal Nuncio was a jolly fellow and when I said that I was impressed by his beautiful robe, he laughed and said in his unmistakably Neapolitan French; " Madame, c'est la première fois qu'on m'a fait des compliments sur ma robe. (Madame, that is the first time that anyone has paid me compliments on my dress!)" Further mirth, and the evening which had shown signs of being extremely boring, turned out to be one of the best ever. As the guests were leaving, the Swiss Ambassador asked us to wait a bit as he wanted to tell us something; he sent the last of his guests off and returned, took my hands in his and said: "Françoise, you are brilliant and if it had not been for you, this whole evening would have been a total bore. Thank you so much for your help" and after that we were reinvited on numerous occasions. These dinners were always excellent as he had the best chef of all the embassies in Brussels.

There was a colleague of Guy's called Johnny Baddeley, who had a dreadful Greek wife, Maria, who was at least ten years older than him. She exasperated everyone and especially me no end. One day she was hurt by a Venetian blind falling on her – an experience not to be wished on anyone. I, in my colourful English, related this story to a friend: "Poor Maria, she was struck by a blind Venetian the other day. You should see the wound!" This was just one of the linguistic mishaps which have always been with me and they still go on. I will mention a few here because they do not really fit anywhere else; even I can see that they are funny. A friend of Guy's used to record them in a little book called "Françoise she say, Françoise she mean" but, unfortunately, someone stole it from his car in Italy.

a) Walking in the Alps on a very hot day and wishing to get my legs tanned, I rolled my shorts up even shorter into hot pants and said: "If you see someone who come the other way, tell me and I take my trousers down" (The first person we met was a monk);

b) "I asked him to cut the bread with his sewing machine" (I was thinking of sawing);

c) Putting my head round the kitchen door in a friend's house to explain why the preparation of a fondue from grated cheese was taking so long, I announced: "Jean-Pierre has three of us here in the kitchen but only one thing to rape with" (the French word "raper" means to grate);

d) Explaining a very hurried journey on foot I said: "I put my legs around my neck and went to the post office to catch the last collection" (straight translation of "prendre ses jambes à son cou" meaning to run very fast);

e) In a discussion with friends in which the falling of educational standards to that of the lowest common denominator was being deplored, I announced that "Schooling is being levelised by the bottom.";

f) In recent years I have taken to cutting Guy's hair now and again, because the local barber often cuts it – what is left of it – too short. One day I stood back to admire my handiwork and noticed that I had left him with a bit of a tuft each side. This obviously had to be corrected and I said: "I will degrade you tomorrow morning", meaning make it slope gradually to his neck.

Guy attributes these mishaps to my approach to language, which, he says, is purely phonetic: I try to make the right noises and I still unconsciously translate literally from French. That conclusion, plus Viennese tradesmens' tendency to agree with what the customer says, produced the most hilarious results during our posting there, e.g. the delivery at the door of a whole dead lamb when I was expecting a leg, to be served at a dinner party about two hours later.

Poor Maria figured later in another absurd incident. Being Greek, unsurprisingly, she was very dark – and hairy to boot. After dinner one summer evening at the Sykes's house, (Richard Sykes was our Head of Chancery; he and Guy had met in the army) she was sitting on the sofa and had no stockings on and the long black hairs on her legs were very much in evidence and most off-putting. To provide some camouflage, I sat on a pouffe in front of her and tried to move as necessary to obscure the view for anyone with whom she became engaged in conversation. Next day I had a stiff neck.

During our stay in Brussels we met Peter Townsend, who was the Air Attaché and not yet married. Everyone was all over him because of his relationship with Princess Margaret and he was the centre of attention, which he enjoyed. I got to know him in a totally different context, away from the limelight of the Embassy, and found him a charming man who loved horses and who was very pleasant and natural with the trainers of the race horses. It was very strange to see the two very different sides of a person with two such contrasting personalities. It was thanks to Townsend that I was able to continue riding and we used to go out very early in the mornings, at five or so, to train them. These horses were neurotic and very sensitive and would bolt at the slightest unusual sound; this made the rides in the forest of Soignes very exhilarating and was an experience I shall never forget. However I did not continue it for very long as often it was hard to get up so early after some of the official parties the night before, when, needless to say, I had over indulged in the liquid department and the heavy head would not take too kindly to being shaken up.

We were also good friends with Count Albert Aponyi, who was a scion of the well-known Hungarian family of that name. He was a delightful but unreliable individual with a constant hole in his wallet, especially at the end of the month. Regularly towards the middle of the month we would get a telephone call from him and we knew it would be he, to fish for an invitation to a meal – which he usually got. He had a weak head for drink and one day mistook Guy's serviette ring for an ash-tray and stubbed his cigarette out, through it, on the polished table top. He did the rounds among our group of friends so he was fed and no one seemed to get tired of the routine. Mickey and Francine Keating Hill were amongst those friends and we had great fun together. Mickey was the Cross and Blackwell representative in Brussels at that time. He had been a gallant Artillery officer during the WW II but tended to get rather drunk with Aponyi and, in those binges, sometimes became trying. That said, we had a wonderful time, as often, when Guy was not around, we would go to some night clubs, the four of us, specially where we could dance the Hungarian Czardas which is a very fast dance and great fun when one is young and has the energy.

One fine day Albert phoned us and invited us out to dinner to thank us for all the meals he had had at our house. So we went to the Hungarian restaurant in the Brussels International Exhibition. We arrived at the Hungarian tent and Albert made himself known to his fellow countrymen in the band and, before we knew it, we were seated at the best table. I should mention that six months before the exhibition opened the Hungarian Uprising had taken place and Brussels had accepted many Hungarian refugees, but the restaurant, of course, represented the communist Hungarian government.

Nevertheless Albert presented himself as the descendant of an older Count Aponyi, at which all the restaurant staff were at our disposal and the orchestra played primarily for Albert, who requested old Hungarian airs to bring him back to his roots and his family's past, if you will. The moment came to leave and the bill landed in front of Albert. Of course he had paid the orchestra with all his money and he said: "oh Guy, I am so sorry". Guy had anticipated this and paid the bill. Albert was just a trifle embarrassed – but it was typical of him and such fun – yet another memorable evening.

At about this time Albert realised that he would have to work and he got a job selling space for a Charleroi newspaper. The concept of selling space was new to me and I caused confusion among friends by telling them that Albert was "selling spice". He had to find somewhere to live in Charleroi and ended up renting a room in a brothel at a very low rent. The Madame took pity on him and did his laundry for free. Appropriately enough, her name was Albertine.

At a cocktail party one day, Guy had a terrible attack of the hay fever which has bothered him all his life. One of those present was David Moreau, who was at that time working for Beechams and experimenting with their new anti-allergic vaccine. The treatment involved 180 injections, 60 in each spring of three successive years. Guy says he felt like a pin cushion for a long time afterwards. The treatment improved the situation somewhat, but, to cure it, Guy had to wait a few years longer for the invention of antihistamines. David, a very intelligent, humourous and somewhat eccentric polymath, became and remains a good friend. He is a successful writer and commentator. He specialises in picking up businesses which are in a mess and sorting them out: then he gets bored with them and moves on. One thing with which he does not get bored with is flying his small aeroplane all over the place, apparently for preference in most appalling weather.

Improperly looking Prince Albert in the eye.
On the right HM Ambassador, Sir George Labouchère

In the course of official entertainment in December 1957 a gala was organized at the British embassy for the Belgian Red Cross. All the members of the embassy were naturally invited to this festive event. The king's brother, Prince Albert, was the patron and therefore guest of honour. As a result, all the women had to be presented officially to him and there was even a rehearsal to establish the order of precedence of the introductions. At the gala itself the Prince was surrounded by the press; when my turn came to be presented at the last moment I improperly lifted my head up, instead of looking demurely down, and smiled a huge smile. The photographers did the flashes, had a field day and the moment was captured. I should never have looked at him. The next day the Ambassadress phoned me saying: "Françoise, congratulations, you are on the front page the world over smiling at the Prince when curtseying in front of him".

As much as I regretted leaving Berlin, I was quite eager to leave Brussels. The members of the Embassy were congenial enough but it was not a fascinating posting. I hated the way most Belgians spoke French and had to go to Paris about once every three weeks to recover from it and also, I suppose, what did not help was that I nearly died after a bad miscarriage and it took me a year to get over it.

HOME - 1958-62

Our posting home to England, to live in Guy's lifelong home in Gerrards Cross was to last four years. Life back in the homeland after the first two postings was quieter than expected and I missed the entertaining, in the course of which I had discovered I had an ability for and enjoyed cooking and for supervising diplomatic functions. I had enjoyed hiring the right staff and training them to serve exactly how I wanted and when I wanted. I had always done the cooking myself so as to be sure of exactly what I was giving my guests and what Guy, being highly allergic to all crustaceans, could eat. Often when invited out, I would try the entrée first and then quickly catch Guy's eye and give him the OK to proceed; the last thing we wanted was to have Guy falling face first into his plate or falling off his chair.

Guy came back from work one day in early 1959 to tell me that we were posted to Rangoon. He had no desire to go there and also he had been promised two years in England for family reasons. I had announced that I was pregnant and, in a nutshell, that cancelled the posting, much to Guy's relief. Inwardly I would have loved to have gone to experience a totally different way of living but Guy was very opposed to the whole idea for several reasons including my health and was very relieved not to go.

On 29th January 1960 I gave birth to our daughter Jocelyn. The boys were now in boarding school and to have another child just then was a godsend. I had a hard time accepting to let go of my sons and the whole boarding school idea was totally alien to me. In France one just did not send one's children away unless the family was dysfunctional for one reason or other. Inwardly, I was heartbroken to see them go but I had absolutely no power over the situation. That was how it was going to be, whether I liked it or not. Guy and I over the years had many an argument on this matter and when it was time for our daughter to go, she followed suit, much to my agony. Part of the argument was that a stable education in one system was much better than changing schools every two to three years when each of the postings ended. For two terms out of the three an allowance was paid by the government, as private education then, as now, was a considerable expense, and it was the logical solution. Nicholas thrived in boarding school and Jeremy did not. For the former, being constantly occupied was heaven, but for the latter the whole situation was dreadful and he suffered immensely and I felt tremendously sorry for him, yet they both continued their education and took their separate forks in the road and went about their lives in different environments. Jocelyn at first had a tough time in boarding school; she was 8 years younger than Jeremy and so was brought up almost like an only child. It was quite wrenching to see her go at the beginning of each term. However, it was not long before she settled down and ended up enjoying her schooling. All three survived it and two of them have good memories of their school days which they say they would not have traded for anything else. Jeremy, who enjoyed only his last few terms at school, was later kind enough to say to Guy; "Pa, you were right. Without it I would never have been able to stand up for myself et on m'aurait marché sur les pieds" (and I would have been trampled on). That has helped him survive the unpleasantnesses of the graphics trade in which he works. I was the one who suffered the most.

Whilst I was spending the usual Houlgate summer holidays we heard that Guy was going to be posted to Vienna. So I decided to look around for a young girl to help me with Jocelyn, rather like an au pair. I found a girl in a small Norman village nearby, the eldest of ten, whose father was a drunk and who was completely exploited by her mother who was overwhelmed by her throng of children. She was an intelligent girl and stayed with us for the duration of the posting. It later transpired that she was quite nasty to Jocelyn and her final days with us were not particularly pleasant as she left the family without warning. She stayed on in Vienna and married an Austrian engineer.

VIENNA - 1962-66

Jocelyn was 2½ when we were posted to Vienna. This was to be a fascinating posting for Guy and I loved it, too.

For accommodation in Vienna we had a rare stroke of luck. Austrian colleagues in Brussels, Heinz and Verena Laube, had been posted home at about the same time as we were and were now to go to Madrid. So they were very happy to rent us their duplex apartment in the centre of town. Everyone was happy and No. 3 Mölker Bastei became our home for four years. It was located just off the Ring, opposite the University, in an old building which originally contained six huge flats. We had part of the top one. The living room was a 7 meter cube with a spiral staircase going up one side to a level where there were three more bedrooms and a large balcony, where Guy and Nick often practiced fencing during the holidays when Nick was home.

That apartment made it possible for us to entertain with ease and many friends and acquaintances were made. Among them I especially remember Fred and Peggy Virski, with whom we have stayed in touch to this day. He had been a Polish cavalry reservist, who fought first the Germans and then the Russians, from whom he escaped to join General Anders's army in the Middle East and was badly wounded at Monte Cassino. She was an American from Virginia and spoke with an appropriate southern drawl. Our paths crossed again later in Geneva. Carlo Calenda, Minister at the Italian embassy, was another memorable character. He became a good friend and we had many a fascinating dinner party with him at our home and his. At that time the only country that had a problem with Austria was Italy – over the South Tirol – and many arguments and discussions about its difficulties with Austrian and Italian colleagues took place in our dining room. Seeing that we were British, we were neutral in this dispute and I like to think that our hospitality may have played some small part in sorting it out.

During these dinners I became good friends with Cetta Franzini, who was married to a much older man, Alberto, who was the representative of Montecatini in Austria. Cetta became an especially close friend of Carlo's and tongues wagged about their romance, of which Alberto was ignorant, in theory at least.

Denise and James McAdam Clark were splendid colleagues in the Embassy. James helped Guy a great deal and Denise and I became very close but, in that very French way, which is incomprehensible to anyone not French, always, until her death, we addressed each other as "vous". They had met at Oxford before the War and Denise was in Paris when it started. She became part of an escape line by which shot down RAF airmen were exfiltrated to Spain and thence to England or North Africa. She kept them in her flat a few days in the course of their perilous journeys. She, like many other such heroes, was denounced, for money of course, by the concierge of the block. She was arrested by the Gestapo and sent to Ravensbrück concentration camp, where she was held for one and a half years; she was one of the fifteen French women survivors of that ghastly camp. She managed to survive because one of the camp doctors at Ravensbrück managed to hide her in a cupboard and gave her aspirin and bits of food when he could. James was an artillery officer throughout the war. He had met Denise's brother before the War and found him again after the Liberation of Paris and together they managed to contact Denise as soon as she was brought back from Ravensbrück and they got her into a sanatorium in Switzerland to recover. Their daughters went to the French Lycée in Vienna and I was very envious of her having her girls at home, while I was allowed my boys only for the holidays as mentioned before.

Paddy and Betty Bolton were a very intelligent, interesting and somewhat eccentric couple and a breath of fresh air in the diplomatic scene. Paddy was for many years Secretary General of the International Atomic Energy Agency. He became and remains a great friend and kindred spirit of Guy's. His wife was killed in a car accident after they left Vienna. We were also responsible for one of our guests meeting his future wife: Count Peter Meraviglia Crivelli, who worked then for the Austrian Institute for Foreign Affairs, and a Swedish diplomat, Countess Görel Palmstierna. They married one year later and live in Germany, where Peter runs a paint business, and we are still in touch.

Another Viennese friend was Willy Hendricks, a charming and very amusing character who might have stepped straight out of a Johan Strauss opera. He had been an officer in the German Abwehr and in Istanbul in 1942 got into mortal trouble (details of which we never found out) with the Gestapo. He managed to escape from them and handed himself over to a member of the staff of the British Embassy there, Nicholas Eliott. Nicholas did not know what to do with him, so locked him in the loo while he made arrangements to evacuate him to Egypt, where he worked for the British until the end of the war. Years later, Guy learnt that Nicholas Eliott's father, Claud, who was the Provost of Eton, had, as a small boy, mistaken Canon Hardwick Drummond Rawnsley, one of the founders of the National Trust, for a burglar and locked him up in the loo at the family house in the Lake District. Nicholas had never heard this story and there was much mirth when Guy told it to him, years after Claud's death. Willy asked us to the annual New Year's Eve gala performance of Die Fledermaus at the State Opera in 1965. The party consisted of Willy and his then wife who was the daughter of Maleta, president of the Senate, Willy's friend Ormond, married to Willy's first wife, Guy and me. Because his wife was who she was, Willy got the box always reserved for VIPs and, as we entered it, a member of the audience, obviously thinking Willy was someone else, began to clap. The whole audience joined in and Willy bowed graciously in all directions, smiled and waved in recognition. This was repeated before each act. After a marvellous performance, we all went to Ormond's house for supper and further mirth ensued when a cracker, intended to explode when I went to the loo, failed to go off. Willy is now on his third wife, who is a delightful Hungarian countess, young enough to be his daughter, and she is a European fencing champion.

In Vienna I had another contretemps with a French diplomatic wife. We were invited to dinner by the French Ambassador and I wore a rather striking white Chanel suit. After nearly all of the guests had arrived, the Ambassadress swept into the room wearing an identical suit, but black. She gave me the dirtiest of dirty looks, did not say "bon soir", stayed just long enough to eat her dinner and then disappeared for the rest of the evening.

Guy had – and still has – another friend in Vienna who is a marine biologist and lymnologist – and, indeed, a remarkable polymath, called Heinz Löffler. Shortly before the end of the WW II, Heinz, as a boy, was conscripted into the German Navy, but he never went to sea because the officers at Cuxhaven discovered that he could draw beautifully and he was employed making greetings cards for their wives and girl friends. At the end of the hostilities he was released and walked back to Vienna. He invented a machine which crawled along the bottom of lakes and ponds to collect samples of the soil. No one in Vienna was interested so, with the proceeds of the sale of a stamp collection, he bought a single ticket to Zürich, took his machine to the University there and obtained help and support which eventually led to the chair of Marine Biology in Vienna University and world-wide recognition as an expert on alkaline lakes. He went to South America, had an appendicitis on the shores of Lake Titicaca and was operated on, without an anaesthetic, by an Indian surgeon. He asked Guy to go with him on an expedition to the Himalayas but Guy could not because it was to take several months. After talking to Heinz afterwards, Guy reckoned that that was all to the good because he would never have survived it. Often at the weekends we went with him to the shores of the Neusiedler See, the most westerly steppe lake, which attracts numerous species of birds. This lake is on the frontier with

Hungary. Heinz was doing some research there and we learnt a lot about this unique area of Austria. It is sandy with lots of vineyards and bird sanctuaries; the birds from all over sojourn there on their migration routes. Some of the Austrian wines grown there are notorious head-ache makers, especially the white; as for the red, it is heavy and fruity and inevitably after consuming even a moderate amount one fell asleep. I tended to fall asleep; Guy was very fond of it.

It came out one day in conversation with Calenda that I was fond of riding and he invited me to ride with him in the Neusiedler See area. To my surprise, a local stable provided very good and beautifully cared-for horses and I experienced, for the first time ever, seeing wildlife of all kinds close at hand. Because we were on horseback and did not talk, animals and birds showed no sign of fear: the fact that humans were present was not apparent to them – we were just part of the – to them – totally unfrightening horses. The memories of that extraordinary place remain with me as fresh as ever.

During our four years in Vienna we served under two Ambassadors, the first was Sir Malcolm Henderson, a charming man who liked Guy; the Ambassador's residence was a divine house with the potential for fabulous parties, but unfortunately both Ambassadors were stingy and the receptions were disastrous, with foul food. The second was Sir John Pilcher, who thoroughly disliked Guy and this was cordially reciprocated. This was the end of going to the residence as we were never invited due to their implacable mutual dislike. This was sad for me as I never set foot in that building again. At that time and for years afterwards the Austrian government was a coalition of Nationalists (conservatives) and Socialists. Pilcher refused to entertain the Socialists and left them to his number two, who sometimes asked us to help.

Vienna being Vienna, we often went to concerts and to the opera. These occasions are still with me today; music played to perfection in such a city is a hard act to follow and inevitably invites invidious comparisons elsewhere.

Cetta and I reckoned that we absolutely had to go to the Opera Ball at least once in our lives and set about organizing a select group of friends to attend this event; this group included David Cornwell (better known as John Le Carré). We had a box and, seeing that Davids' book " The Man Who Came in from the Cold" had just come out, he was quite a celebrity and the press was after him everywhere. The setting with the decor and glittering lights reflecting off all the beautiful dresses and the music with acoustics which could not be better all made a magnificent occasion and left me with a souvenir still crystal clear in my mind. An unforgettable evening if ever there was one.

During our cocktail parties Jocelyn always perched up at the top of the spiral stairs and watched intently, as if not to miss anything, until the nanny came to put her to bed. It was on one such occasion that one of the guests, a Russian, noticed her. She had just started to squint in one eye and he said to Guy: " You know, in Russia we could fix her eyes; it could be done very quickly in Kiev. We could fly her there and we would fly you there too" We did not take up the offer. I took Jocelyn to London shortly afterwards to have her eye put straight at Moorfields Hospital. She was operated on her fifth birthday. A few days, later Guy met this Russian in the street and he said: " How is you little daughter?" Guy said that she was in London and had had the operation the previous day. "And have you news?" asked the Russian and Guy said that he had not yet, at which the Russian said: " Mr. Bratt, in Russia we have telephone".

When we were newly wed, Guy used sometimes to tell me about some of his war experiences. One such incident continued during our posting in Vienna. After the end of hostilities, when Guy was stationed in Nienburg an der Weser and was frantically trying to organise the repair of German Post Office telephone and telegraph lines in the Province of Hanover and Land of Oldenburg (NW Germany), primarily for military use and later for civilian use as well, he was acutely conscious of not having enough resources in Royal Signals troops. He discovered that two complete German Signal Regiments were prisoners of war in Schleswig-Holstein. As these troops, like their British counterparts, included many Post Office engineers and as they had managed to keep most of their transport, Guy suggested to the Chief Signals Officer that they, without any officers of the rank of captain or above, should be brought to Nienburg, put under his command and put to work on the repairs. This was agreed. One of the German officers, Oberleutnant Alfons von Wunschheim, who purported to be an Austrian, offered himself as liaison officer and interpreter. Guy told him that he did not need an interpreter but, if Wunschheim wanted to be the channel for orders, this would be acceptable and so it was for months. Wunschheim asked one day if he could borrow Guy's technical dictionaries and in due course he returned them with his visiting card which read: "returned with many thanks, Alfons Reichsritter von Wunschheim" (Reichsritter being a rank – I think the lowest – in the pre-war German hierarchy of nobility). Guy thought it was just a little bit impressive that, in a unit which genuinely had had some pretty horrific experiences in the Russian campaign, was a man who could still produce a visiting card. In due course those German troops were allowed to go on leave. Wunschheim went on leave – to Austria – and never came back. Guy was naturally furious and wanted the Military Police sent after him but eventually agreed that it was not worth the effort and expense. The work went on satisfactorily, was completed and everyone was in due course demobilized. Years passed.

Shortly after we arrived in Vienna the Ambassador asked us to dinner and Guy found himself sitting next to one Baron Beck, an Austrian and a former German Signals officer. In conversation about the campaigns in Russia, Guy heard place names he had heard before from Wunschheim, so he asked Beck if, perchance, he knew the former. Beck replied that Wunschheim was one of his oldest friends and proceeded to tell the story, absolutely accurately, of what happened at the end of the war and then added that Wunschheim had always been ashamed of what he did and had it on his conscience. Beck then asked Guy why he was so interested – and you can imagine the answer to that. Beck said: " You must meet him again" to which Guy readily agreed and a dinner date was fixed. Guy and I wondered what would happen: obviously Guy was the last person Wunschheim would want to meet but he would look ridiculous to his friend Beck if he refused.

While we were changing for that dinner, I asked Guy how he was going to play it. " Off the cuff," he said, "is the only possible way." We duly went to Beck's beautiful flat on the Ring and rang the doorbell. Beck opened the door himself and we could see through a large hall into another room where Baronin Beck, Wunschheim and his wife were beside a large log fire. Guy strode into the room, thumped Wunschheim on the chest and said: " Schuft, das hat mir 19 Jahre benötigt, Dich wieder zu haben" (Scoundrel, it has taken me 19 years to catch you again) Guy spent the evening reminding Wunschheim of things he had no wish to hear; Wunschheim's wife spent it apologizing to me for her husband's behaviour– family loyalty etc. The outcome of all this was that we saw the Wunschheims now and again, even though Guy always considered him an unreconstructed Nazi; they had a splendid house near Linz, where the biggest room was given up to the heads and antlers (where appropriate) of all the animals he had shot on his hunting expeditions. Guy noticed that Wunschheim was addressed as " Herr Baron" by the locals, so either he had promoted himself or they were being rather typically obsequious. However, his eldest daughter, Baronin Marielies Haerdtl, became my closest Austrian friend and we are still in touch. Her husband, a charming and amusing man, has been involved most of his life with administering the Vienna Musikverein and beautifying its concert hall. For a time he also ran a gramophone record company but then sold it and started manufacturing lavatory seats. " Not much different" he said, "they are both round and have holes in."

We met a very likable architect named Gabriel who lived just outside Vienna, in Klosterneuburg, where he and his wife had knocked two old cottages together to form a delightful house with a large music room. On the walls hung every sort of stringed instrument from a dancing-master's single-stringed fiddle to an enormous doublebase. Like so many Austrians, he was irrepressibly musical and could play them all; his friends, a typical Viennese mixture of professional and amateur musicians, were asked to come there to play chamber music and one of his friends was Nikolaus Harnoncourt, who in the intervening years, has become a well-knowned conductor and specialist in eighteenth and early nineteenth century music. We were invited now and again to these delightful, light-hearted performances at which Harnoncourt would sometimes produce, in manuscript, works which he just discovered and the immensely competent group would play them at sight. The rare mistakes were received with much hilarity: everybody went back a few bars and resumed. On one of these occasions everyone waited in vain for the horn player. Eventually his wife phoned and Gabriel's wife took the call and reported: " Der Peter kommt nicht; er ist b'soffen" (Peter is not coming; he is absolutely blotto) and the program had to be changed. Gabriel was a teetotaler but organized a wine growers' festival every year at Retz, a small town near the Czech border, with a strangely hot microclimate. One September day Guy announced that the following weekend we had to go there to represent the Ambassador at the wine growers' festival. We arrived and settled on our seats overlooking the square. Then came a procession of floats depicting grape cultivation and wine making, accompanied by girls dressed in national dress and a band. It was quite a scene; there were two fountains in this square, which we soon realised did not pour out water but one red wine and the other white. Needless to say, the participants and spectators became very merry. It was a glorious, hot, breezy day and there was a genuine feeling of happiness in the air. The Landeshauptmann (governor of the province) was a charming and friendly fellow and was delighted to have some British guests. Sadly he fell dead the next week.

Following are a few more events worth recounting which took place during our posting in Vienna. The number two in the British Embassy whilst we were there was an able and charming man who had a beautiful but incredibly stupid wife. They threw a cocktail party for the conductor Bernstein, who came to Vienna to conduct some concerts. At one point I saw and heard her asking Bernstein if he could recommend a good window-cleaner. I believe she had no idea that she was talking to the guest of honour. I saw Bernstein's face change to an incredulous expression and took it upon myself to rescue him from the insult. I swooped over and removed him and left the poor woman standing alone, not quite sure what had just happened to her at her own party. This was only one of the many blunders which did her husband's career no good at all. Another notable one (at a time when the Austrian government was a coalition of Nationalists and Socialists) was when this couple had a luncheon for the Socialist journalists. A

Labour government had just come into power in England and the wife blurted out: " Now in England we have a government run by those awful Labour people." The icy silence which followed summed up the extent of her gaffe and I do not believe she noticed it. Yet another splendid blunder was perpetrated at their dinner table when there was a discussion about the Nationalists and Socialists and she proclaimed: " Of course Germany before the war had a Socialist government, but they were National Socialists."

As mentioned before, one of our friends was the Italian minister Carlo Calenda. He was an intelligent man who spoke very fluent French, as if from the south of France, but he had difficulty with Germanic languages. He always started talking English to Guy and gradually and unintentionally slipped into German. Guy always slipped with him, just for fun, and Carlo was always furious when he realised what had happened. He invited us on numerous occasions to his house and to magnificent receptions and dinners. He entertained admirably and had a fabulous cook. His home was vast. The dining room had dark red velvet hangings and Venetian glass chandeliers. Quite staggering. The waiters were dressed like in the old days of livery, in red velvet, white gloves and white stockings and the table setting was always immaculate and uniquely done. His wife loved Rome too much and stayed there during his various postings, so he was always alone until he started to ask my good friend Cetta to preside with him at these dinners. He also asked me and an Austrian baroness who had a crush on him to share this duty but he had no desire to divorce and he enjoyed the life he had framed for himself, with the distant wife and therefore the freedom which came hand in hand with his sporadic celibacy. I keep fond memories of those wonderful evenings.

Being so enthusiastic about horses throughout my life, Vienna offered me a splendid opportunity to see the Lippizaners in the Riding School. At one of the diplomatic functions I met Colonel Handler, who was at that time the director of the Riding School, and during the conversation he learnt of my interest in horses, so it was thanks to him that I got to see these horses close up and learn about their training. I would go to the dressage training and the setting was quite breath-taking. Imagine, if you will, an indoor riding school lit by chandeliers and the riders in perfectly pressed uniforms dating back to the early 19th century, as if time had stopped. He had a charming wife who was a school-teacher and two of her subjects were English and Latin. It transpired that she had heard of Winnie the Pooh so Guy lent her his copy of the Latin version.

Guy, being a Mozart music buff, made sure he did not miss any of the Mozart operas at the Vienna State Opera and the Redoutensaal during our posting in Vienna. The outings to the opera were invariably followed by a dinner at the Sacher Restaurant opposite; this place was and is renowned for its Sacher Torte, a sinful chocolate cake. The staff at Sachers were marvellous and always ridiculously obsequious and addressed Guy as "Exzellenz", which embarrassed him somewhat until he realised that they did this to every diplomat whom they knew.

By way of complete contrast, the Hofburgkeller was a large cellar restaurant in which one sat at large tables and ate quite good but undistinguished food. There was a zither player, whose repertoire inevitably included the Harry Lime tune. That restaurant was fun but at times it tended to get rather full of vulgar, noisy and insensitive tourists, who had neither manners nor sense. One evening, a particularly obnoxious French group made me so angry and ashamed that I got up, stalked across the whole restaurant, according to Guy looking like a thunder-cloud, and told them exactly what I thought of them and their behaviour. They were so surprised to be cursed in their own language that they shut up. The – for me – totally unexpected result was that the Viennese clientele, on getting up to go when they had finished their meals, all came past our table and either thanked me or bowed and smiled.

HOME 1966-70

We were posted back to England for four years. By that time our elder son, Nick, had started at St. John's College, Oxford, and I was enchanted to go and visit him. The architecture alone was a visual treat. I ate a few times in the dining hall, in which the decor had not changed in hundreds of years. In French universities there is no equivalent of this type of setting and I enjoyed those occasions immensely. Nick, like most of the other students, went around on a bicycle and his was none other than my war-time Peugeot bicycle. That bicycle had seen many things in its life until it was stolen from outside one of the colleges. It was almost immediately found as nobody else had one like it. He lived for two years in college and for the last one in a house at Milton Common which he shared with three friends.

During this time in England, Carlo Calenda wrote to me from Tripoli, where he was by then Italian Ambassador (this was just after King Idris died and before Quadaffi came to power), saying that his staff bored him and that all the Italians remaining in Libya were fascists and he hated them; would we please come to entertain him? Guy growled at first, saying that he did not fancy the role of court jester, but I eventually persuaded him by agreeing to spend a few days in Malta on the way. We had to find somebody to look after Jocelyn, who was at that time a day-girl at Maltman's Green School in Gerrards Cross. My parents accepted to come to Gerrards Cross. My father started feeling really ill and it was sad to see him suffering. I asked them to come for two weeks, but they had to stay an extra week because Carlo asked us to help him with a dinner party. Carlo's residence was the splendid former palace of the Italian Governor General when Libya was an Italian colony. The domestic staff were exclusively male, consisting of two Arab man-servants, the former French chef of the French Ambassador to the Vatican and the Egyptian gardener. For the servants the presence of a seasonably scantily clothed woman was too much to bear and they kept trying to touch me whenever they could. That was almost too much to bear, as well. We lived in ridiculous style, with the three of us at one end of an immensely long table in the dining room, eating and drinking the most delicious food and wine, and Carlo lent us his spare Alfa-Romeo to move around in. Unfortunately it did not have 4-wheel drive and Guy did not dare to take it off metalled roads, which was a pity. However, we visited the Roman ruins of Sabratha and Leptis Magna with Carlo; we wished that we had been able to spend more time in both but Carlo had been there often before and we sensed that he was becoming impatient to get out of the scorching sun and back to his comfortable cool residence. Guy discovered that, all through the war, there had been a telephone line from the Department of Antiquities in Rome to their office at Leptis Magna. Carlo wanted me to be his hostess at a farewell dinner which he was going to give for the British Ambassador, who had just been posted to Ankara and who had been very kind to Carlo when he (Carlo) arrived in Tripoli. He also asked Guy to write him a speech in English for the occasion. He then could be seen walking up and down the garden, learning it by heart. On the evening he was word-perfect but all the pauses – the punctuation – were in the wrong places and it was terribly difficult to keep a straight face. However, the evening was a great success, the British Ambassador responded most graciously – and we agreed with Carlo's opinion of his Italian compatriots in Libya.

Jeremy was by this time at Shiplake College near Henley-on-Thames, and Jocelyn boarding at Maltman's Green School, Gerrards Cross. Both schools are typical English private schools, with their goal of producing true English products at the end of the day.

GENEVA AND HOME - 1970-74

Then in 1970 we were off again and this time to Geneva. I was saddened to leave my daughter in boarding school but that was how it was going to be. We lived in a very "sixties" concrete villa on the shore of the Lake of Geneva. It was a fabulous party house with an area of grass (not to be classified as a lawn) going down to the water's edge and a jetty running out into the lake. This house was not beautiful from the exterior but, as it was perched on an incline, the views from inside, both by night and by day, were most attractive. The appearance and colour of the surface of the lake were constantly changing due to the variations of light and shade and there is something remarkably soothing about letting one's eyes skim along the surface of water. Each season the lake took on another personality, from the angry overcast to the bright and clear. Although it was not very clean, we actually swam in it, too. Like one of our previous homes, this house had a story. It turned out that the previous owner was washed up dead on one of the beaches further south towards Geneva. He was known to be a bit of a party animal but no-one ever conducted further investigations into his death and to this day it is assumed that he was drunk and just fell in – walked off the end of the jetty perhaps.

I was not in a happy state of mind but for distraction we threw many parties and I was lucky to go riding frequently in spring and summer on the horse of the French Ambassador to the European Office of the United Nations. Guy was always very busy. We made good use of our flat in Anzère, in the Valais; I spent most week-days there and came back to Geneva for the week-ends' quotas of entertainment.

So it was in 1972 that we returned to England. Jocelyn was twelve and was now at Tudor Hall, a school in Oxforshire. Tudor Hall was run by a woman who had been in Intelligence during the war, became a JP after it and then was persuaded to take a grip on a school which had rather lost its way. She sorted it out with determination and energy and Jocelyn was happy there and made a number of friends with whom she is still in touch.

WASHINGTON - 1974-77

It was two years later, in 1974, that Guy was posted to Washington. He was delighted. The Washington Embassy was and remains huge, friendly and efficient. We again served under two Ambassadors, first Sir Peter Ramsbottom, a delightful, highly-experienced professional officer, who looked and sounded the part (which is very important in the USA) and secondly Peter Jay, a political appointee, whom Guy considered an ass who did not know how to behave. It was at this point that my life took a turn for the worse. In September my mother was knocked down by a car in Paris. An impatient driver just ploughed straight into her, on a pedestrian crossing, projecting her into the air, to land on the pavement with multiple wounds and fractures. My old father was by then quite frail, and my mother was transported to various hospitals around Paris. During the subsequent years mine was the only shoulder either of them could lean on because my brother, as I have mentioned above, having been badly wounded after landing in the South of France with the French Commandos, was never the same again and had married an unspeakably evil woman who turned him totally against our parents. My mother had to have one leg amputated above the knee and then my father died slowly and painfully of a final bout of cancer. My mother returned home minus a leg to her usual life, totally undeterred by her handicap, and expected to continue as if nothing had happened. She started driving again (a DAF propelled by rubber bands) after a forty-year gap, as my father had driven her everywhere before.

She went through 22 "nurses" and so-called "carers", each worse than the one before, and drove me to the edge of a nervous breakdown. She finally died in 1993 aged 98, 19 years after her accident, and during all those years my daughterly duty got the better of me and I sacrificed my life for her at the expense of my own family. That said, it meant that Guy went to his new posting alone, for me to join him six months later. He never complained, thinking it quite natural and horribly sad. He was very busy all the time, supported by an admirable assistant and two excellent secretaries in turn.

He had been allotted a modern, practical and characterless house in Bethesda, on the edge of Kenwood Golf course. You would think that I would have been delighted, but at the first glimpse of the place, I hated it. The whole posting, though fascinating for Guy, was hell for me with only a few memorable events. I was worrying all the time about what was happening to my mother because there was no-one else to share the burden.

However, Washington brought, even to me, three good things. The first was to drive with Guy, Jeremy and Jocelyn over 14,000 miles around the States (south, then west to the Pacific, north into Canada and back to Washington D.C.). The second was that we caught up with friends, British, Canadian and American, with whom we had served on previous postings. Richard Sykes and Guy were at the Royal Signals OCTU together and afterwards met sporadically while soldiering. When we were posted to Brussels in 1956 Richard and his wife Ann were already there and the same happened in Washington, where Richard was

Minister in the Embassy. The third good thing was golf, which I started there and have continued with enthusiasm ever since; I have made a number of good friends in the Denham Golf Club where I play. Guy and Richard were each godfather of the other's daughter. At the end of their posting, the Sykes family went back to London for a time and then Richard was appointed Ambassador in The Hague. Guy went to stay a few days with them and, the day after he left, Richard was shot by the INLA, a IRA splinter group. That was a very sad year for Guy because he lost five of his best friends, one assassinated, one suicide, two wrongly diagnosed (one in Luxembourg and the other in England) and one of cancer.

Guy's Washington posting included the American Bicentennial, the end of the Watergate scandal, a presidential election and the Queen's visit. That visit was a splendid example of something at which the British excel: the planning was tremendous and the execution of a full and complicated programme, under the direction of Col. John Mottram, Royal Marines, the chief of Staff to the Defence Attaché, was carried out with masterly exactitude. A great reception was held in the Embassy garden and mercifully the rain held off for just long enough. I shook hands with the Queen, who was, as usual, wearing one of her outrageous hats, but against the flowers and all the decorations one did not notice her attire and the event was a grand performance indeed.

With Guy, being presented to HM The Queen at the British
Embassy in Washington in 1975

At a reception at the White House shortly after
his election, Jimmy Carter and his wife met diplomatic
wives. While standing in line, I noticed that the First
Lady had taken her shoes off and was standing there
bare-bunion-footed. I and many other wives were
flabbergasted, but when I afterwards said so, I was told
by Lady Ramsbottom that I was being stuffy and must
get used to American informality.

I became very good friends with the British
Commercial Minister's wife, Elisabeth Cortazzi, and
thanks to her my life in Washington was made bearable.
We have remained friends ever since and, on returning to
England after Guy's posting ended, we met again in
London before they went to Tokyo, where Hugh, an
outstanding Japanese scholar and speaker, was appointed
Ambassador. Elisabeth asked me to modernize her

dresses, as she would be entertaining a lot and attending many official functions. This was fun for me and gave me something else to focus on; it reminded me of the war-time years and having to be creative with existing material. The burden of my mother was heavy for me for all those years and preyed on my mind so much that a full seven years are a black passage in my memory. Today's demographics are showing what I had already experienced. The older generation and their demand for continuing life play a nasty role on the next generation's assessment of guilt: should they stand back and let these aged persons rot away in some expensive nursing home or should they take it upon themselves to care for them in whatever way possible? I believe I did what was right and a sense of pity made me even more determined not to let this poor being wither away in loneliness.

ROUND THE WORLD – OCTOBER-DECEMBER 1978

When we left Washington in 1977, and Elisabeth Cortazzi, told me that she and her husband would soon be posted back to London and, shortly after that, they would be posted to Tokyo, I said that I would call on them there, once they were well established, Elisabeth said that would be splendid, but I ought to bring a friend because she would be very busy and not be able to look after me all the time.

When I mentioned this to my elder son Nicholas, he suggested that, instead of returning westwards from Japan I should continue eastwards and go round the world. I gave this idea a lot of thought and realised that I must, first, find someone to go with me and, secondly, decide exactly where I wanted to stage on this trip. I found out that at that time Singapore Airlines were offering a wonderful deal, a round-the-world ticket, with several short breaks along the way.

In summer 1977, as usual, I was in Houlgate in Normandy with our children and, as usual, met some of their friends who were the children of old friends of mine. One day, on the beach, I was talking to a friend, Marie-Claude Despierres, whose husband had just died suddenly, aged 52, of a brain haemorage and I happened to mention my idea of a trip around the world. Her three children came to see me later that day and asked if I would consider taking their mother with me because it would do her a lot of good in her state of terrible shock. Marie-Claude is two years younger than me, speaks no English at all and had never been further from Paris than the Massif Central. She was very keen to come and I said it would have to be on my terms; I would do all the planning; the trip would take about 8 weeks; she would have to go where I wanted to go; once the arrangements were made, she would not be able to change them. All this she was happy to accept. I got down to the detailed planning. Among the possible stops there were to be 10 essentials: Bombay; Kuala Lumpur (to accept a pressing invitation from the Malaysian Chinese parents of my daughter Jocelyn's school friend, Ruby Lau); Singapore (because the airline insisted on 3 nights in a very good hotel there); Hong Kong; Tokyo (to stay with the Cortazzis); Taipei (to see the marvellous museum which houses all the priceless ivory, gold, jade, etc. treasures which Chang Kai-Check brought to Taiwan when the Communists drove the Kuomintang out of mainland China; San Francisco (to stay with Jacqueline Dentan, a childhood friend); Mexico City (an extra, added to the round trip ticket, to see my younger son, Jeremy and his Mexican wife, Mónica, who were living there at that time; Washington (to see several American friends and colleagues from our previous postings); New York (to see my elder son, Nicholas, and his Japanese wife, Kuniko who live there).

The whole exercise was fascinating and most rewarding and I shall always remember much of it as clearly as if it had happened last week. A lot of it, on the other hand, would be excessively boring to anyone who knows the places concerned, but I will mention some incidents which were out of the run-of-the-mill tourist experiences.

We started out from London mid-October 1978 and everything went more or less according to plan, with the addition of some unforeseen episodes. In Bombay, our first stop, we got off to a bad start. For the journey from the airport to our hotel we were unfortunately inveigled into an "unofficial" and bogus taxi. After about half an hour, our driver purported to have a puncture, in the middle of nowhere in particular, said that he had no spare wheel and refused to give us our luggage back unless we paid him a lot more money than the agreed fare for the whole trip. It was extremely hot and the place where our evil driver had stopped stank to high heaven. Interested locals began to close in around us and we became quite panicky. Fortunately another taxi with a foreigner in it came along and stopped when the driver saw me waving frantically. Even more fortunately, he joined in the dispute with our driver and was entirely on our side. After some considerable argument, the "ransom money" for our luggage was talked down to a reasonable amount and the passenger in the second taxi, an American, kindly allowed us – and our luggage – to join him in it and go on to Bombay. The second driver explained this was a fraud to which likely-looking foreigners were often subjected by bogus taxi drivers – and what easier-looking victims than two unaccompanied women? We were very lucky and thanked our rescuers most sincerely.

In the hotel in Bombay there were a lot of Middle Eastern men, apparently on some sort of group tour. They tried to get into our room but fortunately we could lock the door, so they had to content themselves with trying to look through the key-hole. When it began to rain some of them went outside the building to stand in the rain, got soaked and apparently enjoyed it greatly.

On the first day of our 2-day stay in Bombay we took a boat to Elephant Island, where the only elephants are stone ones, and on the second we visited a dairy farm about 40 miles outside that very unpleasant city. Then on to Singapore and what a contrast that was, so beautiful, tidy and clean; like Switzerland, only more so except for the very hot and humid climate. The government is very strict, for example, if a youth has long hair, he is immediately arrested.

We had decided to go by train from Singapore to Kuala Lumpur and we ran into trouble at the Malaysian frontier which I ought to have foreseen. This was at a time when the Malaysian government was in a very anti-British mood ("Buy British Last" was the slogan written on every suitable surface). I was told that, because I had a British passport, I needed a visa; Marie-Claude, with her French passport did not. I argued for half an hour, telling the immigration official that we were travelling together and if I was not allowed in, she would not be able to travel either. Eventually I said: "We are going into your country and we shall spend some money. If you do not let us in, the money will not be spent there and that would be very sad for you and your country". At that point opposition faded away and we were allowed in. Dato and Datin Lau met us at Kuala Lumpur station and took us to their lovely home, on top of Kenny Hill in the outskirts of the city, with a wonderful view over the jungle. It was extremely hot and humid.

Next morning, at breakfast, Datin Lau noticed that I had a bandage around my left hand and wrist (I am left handed) and asked me why. I told her that it was rheumatism and my doctor in England had said: "There is nothing one can do about it; take some aspirin if it hurts". Datin Lau said: " We don't have rheumatism in this country. I will take you to a Chinese healer who will be able to do something for you but you must 'dress down' for the occasion." So the next day, after visiting a rubber plantation, we drove some way from Kuala Lumpur to a remote isolated area, parked the car and walked for ten minutes into the jungle until we came to a small house covered with jungle plants. We went in and saw about ten people, some of them blind, obviously waiting for attention. Datin Lau took me past all of them up to a curtain, which she gently opened. Kneeling on the floor behind it was an old woman with a big basket in front of her. Datin Lau put some money into the basket and said something to her in Chinese, at which she got up and disappeared. A few moments later she came back and signalled us to follow her; we went along a dimly lit, hot and sticky corridor, at the end of which she opened a sliding door. We found ourselves in front of a big Chinaman, stripped to his waist, around which he had a sort of sash. His long black hair was tied in a knot behind his head. There was a young man, whom I took to be a disciple or amanuensis, in one corner of the room, which was lit by two candles between which was an incense burner – all very spooky. We all bowed to each other and Datin Lau told him about my wrist – her presence was essential throughout to translate because he spoke no English. He said: "Whatever is the matter with you, you must come here for treatment every day for two weeks, otherwise it is not worth starting." Datin Lau assured him that I would stay that long. He massaged my hand and wrist in all directions and it was quite painful. He then rubbed them with a horrible-smelling ointment made, he told us, with snake venom. On the morning of the fifth day I awoke with my hand stinging as if I had fallen into stinging nettles. When I went to the healer that afternoon, he asked whether I had had any reaction to his treatment during the previous night. I told him about the nettle sensation. His face broke into a broad smile and he said: " You will be all right now, because I have restored all the blood circulation in your hand and wrist. You will come back for massage on the remaining days of the fortnight and when you leave Malaysia you will take some of my ointment with you and, every night, rub it into your hand and wrist. When it is finished, you will continue the treatment with any sort of greasy ointment. If you do that, you will never have any more pains in your hand or wrist." His final words, when we parted on the last day, were: "If only we could pass to European doctors all our knowledge of this sort and if the European doctors and surgeons could help us, especially with surgey, we could all heal and save so many more patients." I have followed his instructions meticulously ever since (I was quite glad when I finished his wonderful ointment because it had the most awful smell), and to this day, I have never had any more pain in my left hand or wrist. I count myself extraordinarily lucky and will remain eternally grateful to Datin Lau for taking me to her healer.

We had orginally planned to take a plane from Kuala Lumpur to Penang but we decided to go by train, so that we could see the countryside. However, what we did not know – and, in retrospect, it seems odd that the Laus did not warn us – was that the day we were to travel was in the middle of a Malaysian National Holiday, when all families get together to celebrate. The train left Kuala Lumpur at 9 a.m. and was full to burst, went very slowly and stopped everywhere. Fortunately in our compartment there was a young librarian who spoke very good English and told us a great deal about her country and I did the same for her about France and England. I had to work hard because everything she said I had to translate for Marie-Claude. We arrived in Penang at 2 a.m. and our librarian's boyfriend was at the station to meet her. He asked if we had told our hotel to send a car to collect us and, when we told him we had not, he said: " Let me help, I will find you an honest taxi-driver. You must be very careful here, especially two women alone." I began to be very worried but did not say a word to Marie-Claude so as not to frighten her. All went well and we had a half hour drive on a warm night with glorious full moon and no-one about. We arrived at our hotel at 3 a.m. very tired and dirty, to be greeted by the porter who said: "Where on earth have you been? We went to collect you at the airport 24 hours ago". I explained that we had decided to come by train and had no idea that we were definitely expected to come by air. Anyway, this adventure was followed by three days of luxury, warm sea and relaxation. For our return to Kuala Lumpur, one thing was certain: we were not going by train. Again because of the National Holiday, all planes were fully booked, so the only thing to do was to go by taxi.

The hotel manager eventually got us a taxi, which we had to share with a peasant woman, with two chickens and a bird in a cage. About half way to Kuala Lumpur, at Ipoh, the peasant woman got out and disappeared. The driver said he would continue to Kuala Lumpur only if we paid him much more money and went off to a bar. We had no money and, because of the National Holiday, the banks were shut. So there we were in the middle of Ipoh, with no shade, extremely hot and thirsty, not daring to leave the taxi because all our luggage was in it and there was too much for us to carry. After about an hour of wondering what would become of us, we had another extraordinary stroke of luck. A young man came up and asked in excellent English if, by any chance we were going to Kuala Lumpur. It turned out that he was an engineer who had come to Ipoh to see his parents for the holiday and was trying to get back to Kuala Lumpur. On hearing our story he went into the bar and sorted out the taxi-driver and we all set off once more. Marie-Claude and I were terrified during all our return to Kuala Lumpur. The taxi-driver had had too much to drink and seemed to enjoy overtaking cars on bends and roaring with laughter each time he did it – Marie-Claude crossed herself thinking all the time that we would never make it to Kuala Lumpur, and that we would die in a car crash. But we made it. When we reached Kuala Lumpur we dropped off our young engineer where he wished to go and he told the driver to take us to the Palace Hotel. When we got out of the taxi, the Porter, a splendid Sikh with white gloves and immaculately well dressed, looked at us filthy, covered in dust, our clothes all crumpled, as if we had come from another world. He paid the driver and asked if he could help. No doubt, mention of Dato and Datin Lau had convinced him that he would be reimbursed. I asked him to phone them to report our arrival and Datin Lau swiftly arrived, paid him for his pains and took us home amid much mirth.

After a few more days with them, we went to Hong Kong for three days and then to Tokyo, where my friend Elisabeth Cortazzi picked us up at the airport, installed us in the Embassy Residence and put a Mini with driver at our disposal. During our two weeks stay there, Elizabeth took us to various museums and we went to Kyoto and back in the Bullet train which was most impressive. In addition, Akiro Matsui, a retired senior Japanese diplomat and my son Nicholas's father-in-law, took us to a fascinating Japanese theatre and to a formal tea ceremony. The Cortazzis had another guest for part of the time we were there, Sir John Pilcher, a former Ambassador to Japan, whom I knew, of course, from our time in Vienna. In spite of his intense dislike of Guy, he was very kind and helpful to us and took us out several times. I think he had a soft spot for Marie-Claude. It struck me, much later, that the Cortazzis, Pilcher and our Mexican hosts (see below) and Nicholas and his wife were the only people – except me – to whom Marie-Claude could talk French during the whole trip.

We spent 3 days in Taipei, then went to San Francisco, Mexico City, Washington and finally New York.

The only serious mishap during the trip, was when Marie-Claude slipped on the doorstep of the house of one of my American friends and broke her foot. She had to visit New York and come home with her foot in plaster; thank goodness it happened very near the end of the trip. We got home in early December.

HOME - 1978 ONWARDS

Guy had assumed that he would retire after his Washington post but he was asked to concern himself with the dangers of the international proliferation of nuclear weapons for "perhaps a year". He agreed and said of course he would do whatever was required of him but pointed out that he knew nothing about it. That objection was waved aside and he set about learning as fast as he could. In fact, he did it for ten years, travelling all over the world and being totally immersed in the subject. I was very sorry that I was not able to accompany him. Instead I continued golf with enthusiasm and also started playing bridge again. These two activities have brought me more friends in England than I ever had before. Five grand children also ensure that I do not get too pompous and stuffy.

Guy finally retired to a quiet life in Gerrards Cross, content to potter about and give more time to his life-long hobby of model railway building and operating; doing some voluntary work in three groups of the Chiltern Society, a body devoted to the care of his beloved home county, Buckinghamshire; doing a bit of writing on a variety of subjects and quite a lot of DIY work for our house in Gerrards Cross and the family house in Normandy and a little for the flat in Anzère. He travels to Switzerland and France now and again for a change of scene, and to the USA, mainly to see Nick, Jocelyn and their children. Encouraged by the children, he wrote a book, with which he was totally absorbed for three years. It is on a subject surprisingly remote for someone with his background and is called "The Bisses

With Jocelyn on the top of Chamossaire above Anzère
(Valais) in September 1982

With Nicholas (on my left) and Jeremy on top of the
Wildhorn above Anzère (Valais) in September 1981

of Valais". It was the first comprehensive study of man-made irrigation water-courses in one canton of Switzerland since 1871 and the first ever in English. The subject is esoteric and so the book was not and never will be a best seller – but it got good reviews in the Swiss press and was well received by a specialised public in Switzerland, England and elsewhere – perhaps in part due to the concise and lucid style of someone who has spent much of his life writing. It goes on selling quite well.

He travels up to London to go to his club, The Travellers, for lunch or dinner now and again and to catch up with other colleagues, some retired and some still serving. The Travellers Club was founded in 1819 "to enable gentlemen who travel abroad to meet and to entertain distinguished visitors from overseas" and its overseas associations remain strong. It is a friendly place; the food is excellent and I enjoy going there once in a while, sometimes just for a meal and sometimes to attend a lecture as well.

The Travellers offers its members the possibility of renting some of its rather elegant rooms for entertaining large gatherings such as wedding receptions and parties. So, in January 1988, we held Jocelyn's wedding reception in one of these rooms. The setting was ideal to house the hundred-odd guests who came. The wedding and reception preparations took a lot out of me. I actually made her dress which she and I designed and had a Parisian pattern-maker cut out. I also made the bridesmaids' dresses and all these items turned out very satisfactorily but I needed a rest, as needless to say, my mother was still alive and demanding a lot of care on top of everything else.

Jeremy, Jocelyn and Nicholas (on her left) at her wedding at The Travellers Club in January 1988

I went to Anzère to recover which should have been the perfect remedy for tiredness, but unfortunately I broke my leg skiing. I was extremely well looked after and still ski today. However, for the year following the break I was not allowed near the slopes. I heard that my cousin Michel Burnand, his wife and a few friends were going to South Africa and they asked me to join them on the trip. Seeing that skiing was out of the question this was a wonderful idea. So, on the 6th of February 1989 we flew from Paris direct to Johannesburg. The trip organisers were Gérard and Dorothée Walbaum (friends of my cousin's) who had lived most of their lives in Johannesburg. He had been the representative for the French Airline UTA for many years, had just retired and started organising such trips. Upon arrival we were met and ushered into two minibuses which became our mode of transport for the whole trip.

Obviously thousands of tourists visit South Africa and hundreds of books have been written describing the country and its history and its flora and fauna. I am not going to try to cover that ground yet again in any detail. I will simply mention our route and comment on a few things which struck me from a purely personal point of view.

The route was: Johannesburg - Gold Reef City - Pretoria - Kruger Park - Blyde River - Kimberley - Potchefotroom - Karoo Region - Grahamtown - Port Elizabeth - Fort Frederick - The Garden Route - Tsitsikana Forest - Knysna - Outeniqua Pass - Oudtshoorn - French Hoeck - Capetown.

We learned that it was at Grahamtown that the first South African Baptist church was founded and at first there was no segregation of whites and blacks there. In 1812 there were riots and segregation was introduced. However, we were surprised to see how well blacks and whites there seemed to get along. The schools were mixed and the children all wore the same uniform. Indeed, it was the only town we visited where we felt there was no racial animosity at all.

On the Garden Route, on the coast near Knysna, we visited a small chapel where there is a plaque in memory of two brothers, aged 23 and 22, who went to England in 1942 to join the RAF. Both were killed. This hit me in the stomach because it is so immensely sad that this tragedy had to be recorded so far from Europe.

When we arrived at the Cape of Good Hope and discussed our various thoughts about the whole trip, we all agreed how beautiful South Africa is, with its glorious climate, fascinating wildlife and extraordinary vegetation. We certainly understood why the Huguenot refugees from the France of Louis XIV settled down and stayed there after the Revocation of the Edict of Nantes. From the moment of their arrival in the Cape in 1684, they were accepted by the Dutch and British settlers. They were intelligent and worked hard, just as their counterparts did who took refuge and settled in Holland and England. They brought grape vines which throve and improved in the wonderfully favorable climate; some of their wines are as good as, if not better than, some of the wines of France. These Huguenots settled in an area near Stellenbosch which came to be known as French Hoeck. French family and some place names are still to be found there, but the Huguenots quickly became assimilated into the Afrikaner community and use of the French language died out. Some of our party were surprised that people with well-known Huguenot names, like Beaulieu, Aubigné, and Villiers spoke no French at all and were not the slightest bit interested in people who also had

French names. I had realised this before: when we were in Vienna, we had a colleague in the South African Embassy named de Villiers du Buisson, an ancient French Protestant family, but he was a typical Afrikaner, spoke no French and was mildly, politically correctly at the time, anti-British, too.

Nevertheless in 1943 a monument was erected at French Hoek in honour of the Huguenots and its inscription reads "Elevée sur cette terre sacrée en 1943 par le peuple sud-africain en l'honneur des Huguenots du Cap (1684) en reconnaissance de leur apport inestimable à la formation de notre nation" (Erected on this sacred ground in 1943 by the South African people in honour of the Huguenots of the Cape (1684) in recognition of their incalculable contribution to the making of our nation). I must say that, when I saw this monument, situated in a very beautiful setting, I could not help being proud that I also am a Huguenot. Those people have shown great courage, determination and will to survive and the result is a great success.

I was left with a feeling of great sadness for this spectacularly beautiful country. It seemed odd to me that this paradise should have a split society which could not live in harmony with itself. After all, they have everything on their doorstep. This trip was a visual treat as well as quite an education on a part of the world we had never travelled to in the course of Guy's work; I will have lasting memories of such natural beauty.

HEALTH

When I look back – and touch wood firmly with both hands – I think that I was very lucky indeed healthwise. Apart from some mediaeval dentistry, without anaesthetic, in Paris to remove two impacted wisdom teeth when I was 17, my encounters with the medical and dental professions have been gratifyingly successful. A spot on one lung was seen off by Alpine air thanks to our family GP in Paris when I was 16. An English opthalmologist diagnosed a little lump on my right eye-ball as episcleritis (in a form so rare that he had seen only one other case, his own wife) and cured it, over 10 months, with an autovaccine, the preparation of which necessitated the removal of my tonsils and the application of which was so tricky that he insisted on the termination of a pregnancy at 3 months. This treatment undoubtedly saved me from loosing the sight of that eye and he gave me the strictest orders never to let anyone touch the tiny remains of the lump, of the presence of which I am conscious only when I am very tired. A subsequent bad miscarriage was survived thanks to the skill of an English gynaecologist. Twenty-five years of chronic sinus trouble, which began when I was 14 and was declared incurable by an English GP, was sorted out permanently by a specialist in Vienna. "Rheumatism" in my left hand and wrist was cured by a Malaysian Chinese healer, as mentioned above. A bad leg break (skiing) was spectacularly dealt with by a surgeon in Switzerland which involved having a steel plate and 12 screws put inside the leg (all subsequently removed); I only missed one skiing season. Five years of intermittent pain in my right wrist brought about by pulling my mother's wheel chair, with her in it, up kerbs during her long, one-legged existence in Paris was cured through acupuncture by a Chinese doctor in San Francisco. How different my life would have been if any one of these interventions had been ineffectual.

UPON REFLECTION

l look back on my life in those quieter evenings and understand that I have led a very full and interesting life, meeting people from all over the world and from the most varied backgrounds and listening to their view points. This reminds me of one dinner in Geneva at the British Consul General's house, where I was introduced to two members of the staff of the Chinese Mission, dressed identically in the then typical Mao grey suits. These two did not speak a word of English and appeared somewhat withdrawn. I established that they both spoke good French and so I ended up chatting to them, and could not resist asking them: "By the way, are you Madame or Monsieur? you both dress alike and I have no idea who is who". The man, who had a hidden sense of humour smiled, somewhat secretly, and informed me who was who. These people, when I think back, demonstrated to me that evening how lucky we were to be free; they were chaperoned by a similar-looking individual, who was watching their every move, and I felt so lucky to have been born in the West and spent my life with freedom of thought and freedom of movement except during the nightmare years of the German occupation of France. We asked that couple to dinner and the chaperon came too, uninvited. We made a great fuss about laying an extra place at table and then totally ignored him.

Accompanying Guy on his various postings enabled me to understand different cultures and appreciate aspects of my own which I had not considered before. The postings were so different from one another that it is hard to say which was the best. In Berlin we were at a tremendous advantage over the Germans: we had everything we needed, which in turn enabled us to throw the most fun parties and being a hostess suited me fine. In Vienna, where important discussions which did not really concern us took place under our roof, life was fascinating and we were in a position to watch and to listen to lots of marvellous music. Brussels, which was my least favourite posting, still offered me the chance of meeting interesting people like Peter Townsend, and meeting them away from the public eye, showing a very different side of themselves – I was lucky. During the French student uprisings in 1968 we were on holiday in Switzerland and not really made to feel the significance of the movement; once again the Swiss had managed to avoid uncomfortable circumstances and life went on as if nothing was happening. Living in Switzerland, one felt that they were a very blessed people, having never suffered major wars; most were adequately well-off and everything works – in short – nothing to worry about in this most beautiful country.

I helped Guy in his career as much as I could in my capacity and I feel I did a good job. He thinks so, too, and assures me that all of his colleagues who know me do also. The times were very political and it was often awkward to explain what we were doing in whichever country we were living in at that moment. I came to understand and accept my role. I had lived through an eventful period in history from the time in Paris during World War II to the collapse of Communism in 1989.

As I have indicated above, I have been saddened from time to time by the recurring difficulties which arise between France and England. I have to agree with Guy that there is a background of resentment in France at any success or achievement by the British. Salvador de Madariaga in "Portrait of Europe" and Robert Gibson in "Best of Enemies" understood and analysed brilliantly this frame of mind. Having fought each other for centuries, this sentiment ought to be a thing of the past but, in certain circles, it is still there and the fact that Britain has had to come to the rescue of France twice in a life-time has not helped. The other side of this coin is the questions which many Brits and Americans put to themselves and to each other: are the French really worth the losses suffered by both of us while chasing the Germans out of France, twice, after the inadequacies of French governments had enabled them to come in? What sort of gratitude was it to scrawl on any suitable surface, just after the War, "US go home" and for de Gaulle to do his utmost to exclude Britain from the Europe which it had played a major part in liberating? Why do so many French families who have British children to stay brain-wash them to the effect that the British did not really make an important contribution to the winning of the two World Wars? On a more personal level, why is it that, in all these years, Guy has only once received from anyone in France any appreciative words for his seven years soldiering for the common cause? For anyone like me, with one French foot and one Anglo-Saxon one, this sort of thing is profoundly disappointing.

Life for me in England has obviously become much calmer than the previous 35 years of nomadic existence, encountering different environments in different parts of the world, meeting people and watching how they might turn out and seeing how some of them ended up. Now life is settling down to one of comparative leisure and enjoyment of good health, good food and wine, golf, bridge, skiing, being totally awe-struck by all the changes brought about by the technological revolution, and generally watching out for each next new development. Most importantly, I have made a circle of good friends for the first time in England; I never got round to it before, what with overseas postings, coping with our children and what Guy calls an overdeveloped sense of filial piety towards my late parents. The twenty-first century is now with us and I cannot imagine a repeat of my life because it was so specific to a unique period and I became part of the consequence of an era. When I met Guy I was young and fed up with being in France. I ran away from the hardships, needed a change and took an eventful ride which I shall never regret. Had the war never happened I would have married a Frenchman and my life would have been totally different from the one I have had. With luck, I might have been much better off; I would have been much more concerned with "les apparences"; I would have remained much more typically Parisian; I would not have had anything like as much fun.

In the course of long marriages such as ours (57 years to be precise) there have naturally been periods which were very rocky. Having a husband so totally immersed in a working world so far removed from most normal nine to five jobs, life has been sometimes both lonely and trying. There have been periods when I wondered why I gave up so much to support a chap who put his work before everything and ask myself for what in return?

On the other hand, I have been able to indulge my passion for skiing, which I started age 7 and, touch wood, at 76, I am still doing every winter. I am very happy that two of my children and two of my grand children started to ski at about the same age as I did and share the passion. Guy never learned to ski, which was sad for me, but he has always felt that holidays belong to summer and that to have a skiing holiday with a husband who was a beginner would be no fun for me. However, he has been totally understanding of my enthusiasm and even in our poorest days, when he was studying, managed to afford to send me off to the mountains. He loves mountains in the summer and almost every year from the end of WW II until we got the flat in Anzère, we walked great distances, often in rough conditions, in the Austrian and Swiss Alps. Since 1972 the flat in Anzère, with its marvellous view of 100 or so miles of the Penine Alps, has been holiday headquarters much loved by the whole family, including Jeremy who does not ski but loves the mountains and has inherited a large dose of the artistic ability of my Neuchâtelois ancestors and has made wonderful sketches of the mountain scenery. Two of our children, much to my sadness, live far away, their lives very much wrapped up with the changing times. I know that they will always be there to help me out in my ageing years and their support is something I will always be able to count on. Along with all the fun, my life has dealt me some interesting, sad and unusual cards which have allowed me to play through all the hurdles and live a very full life, with health on my side enabling me to make the most of it.

ENVOI

Instinctively trying to find a bit of France abroad, on arrival in London for the first time as a child, I assumed and announced that the figure on the top of the column in Trafalgar Square was Napoleon – thereby giving the taxi-driver an apoplectic fit.

ACKNOWLEDGEMENTS

I am grateful to my daughter Jocelyn, who urged me to write this book and who typed the first two drafts, to my second son Jeremy, who typed subsequent drafts and, with Mónica his wife, designed the cover, to my grandson Guy (13) who searched high and low on the Internet for photographs, to my husband Guy who edited the text and liaised with the printers and to Dr. Audrey Baker who helped with proof-reading.